Teaching Writing in the Content Areas:

SENIOR HIGH SCHOOL

Stephen N. Tchudi, 1942-
and
Joanne Yates

nea PROFESSIONAL LIBRARY
National Education Association
Washington, D.C.

Printing History:

First Printing:	September 1983
Second Printing:	August 1984
Third Printing:	January 1986

Note

The opinions expressed in this publication should not be construed as representing the policy or position of the National Education Association. Materials published as part of the Writing in the Content Areas series are intended to be discussion documents for teachers who are concerned with specialized interests of the profession.

Library of Congress Cataloging in Publication Data

Tchudi, Stephen, 1924-
    Teaching writing in the content areas: senior high school.

    Bibliography: p.
    1. English language—Composition and exercises.
2. Report writing. I. Yates, Joanne Mueller.
II. Title.
LB1631.T27   1983   808'.042'0712   82–24536
ISBN 0-8106-3228-4

CONTENTS

The Authors

Stephen N. Tchudi is Professor of English at Michigan State University, East Lansing.

Joanne Yates is in Special Education, Napa County Schools, California.

The Advisory Panel

Anthony J. Amirante, general science teacher, Los Angeles Unified School District, California

Martha H. Barry, science teacher, McBee High School, McBee, South Carolina

David A. England, Associate Professor, Curriculum and Instruction, West Virginia University, Morgantown

Margaret Parish, Assistant Professor of English, University of North Carolina at Wilmington

August Schau, Resource Teacher, Buckfield High School, Buckfield, Maine

Beverly Schuh, Home Economist, Ashley High School, Ashley, North Dakota

Mary Wadsworth Sucher, Reading Specialist, Baltimore County Reading Services, Maryland

Ray Taylor, retired mathematics teacher, Waynesboro High School, Georgia

Introduction

WRITING IN THE CONTENT AREAS— WHAT IS IT? WHY DO IT?

These days no one seems satisfied with the way Johnny and Jane write: not parents, not school administrators, not the media, not teachers, not even Johnny and Jane themselves. There are no cure-alls for this "literacy crisis," but one of the most exciting ways for teachers to help their students become more effective writers is through writing in the content areas: using language as the medium through which subject-matter learning takes place.

Of course, all writing has content. One can no more write without content than make an omelet without eggs. This publication suggests, however, that teachers be concerned not only with the language children use to express academic content, but with the accuracy of the content as well; that writing skills be sharpened on subject-matter projects, not just on isolated language arts exercises.

The relationship between language and content is not a recent discovery. The Greeks, insisting that the rhetorician be knowledgeable in many fields, saw the good public orator as one who could skillfully and persuasively marshal arguments on a wide range of subjects. During the Middle Ages, interest in content and language was revived; the language subjects of *grammar*, *rhetoric*, and *dialectic* (or logic) in the medieval curriculum were said to underlie such content-area disciplines as mathematics and natural science. In our own time another revival of interest in content-area writing is occurring. English/language arts specialists have observed that writing skills taught in isolation from content are not likely to be learned successfully. Students need to apply their language skills to real communications tasks, including writing in science, geography, social studies, mathematics, and vocational and career education.

Writing can also offer a teacher ways of eliciting information that are far more interesting to students (and teacher) than conventional examinations. For example, when studying the Amazon River Basin, the teacher who has students write vividly about an imaginary journey up the Amazon will help them understand the river in ways missed by the teacher who merely has them fill in blanks on an answer sheet. Similarly, when students write imaginatively about scientific principles—say, using their knowledge from a unit on fuels to write a futuristic story about transportation—they will learn their subject more effectively than when they merely master the basic

5

concepts in the textbook.

Writing is a practical skill, one of the most useful a student can learn, but it is valuable for more than classnotes, examinations, and research reports. Writing in the content areas can transform notetaking—the writing down of facts to be remembered—into journal keeping, when students interact with and respond to subject matter content. It can turn the traditional unit on the business letter into a real exercise in communication when students write genuine letters to live people in an attempt to learn something for class. It can change examination writing from regurgitation to imaginative synthesis and integration of ideas.

The claims of writing in the content areas to be part of the curriculum are many, but those that follow articulate some of the most persuasive reasons for all teachers to attend to the teaching of writing as well as to the teaching of content or subject matter.

1. *Writing about a subject helps students learn better.* The outcome of content writing programs is not simply improved language skills (an important end in itself), but improved learning of subject matter. If writing provides opportunities for students to play with ideas and concepts, then students will come to understand the subject more richly and deeply than before.

2. *Writing about content has practical payoff.* Perhaps the biggest reason Johnny and Jane do not write well is that they have not had enough practice doing it. Teachers whose students write frequently on content-area topics are providing a great service to those students, including short-term payoff (better writing of school papers) and long-range rewards (becoming successful writers at higher levels of education and in the real world).

3. *Content writing often motivates reluctant writers.* English compositions are often badly written because the topics are bland and banal: "My Summer Vacation," "The Most Unforgettable Character I Ever Met." Many so-called nonwriters are merely writers waiting for an engaging content-area topic to come along: *computers, science, history, futurism.* Writing about content gives substance to student writing and helps inspire many inexperienced and previously unmotivated writers.

4. *Content writing develops all language skills.* Although the principal concern here is writing, language skills are so tightly interwoven that a better title for this publication might be *Teaching* Literacy *in the Content Areas: Reading, Writing, Listening, Speaking.* The model units demonstrate this by including supplementary reading, questions for talk and discussion, and even opportunities for drama and media composition.

5. *Teaching writing teaches thinking.* According to an old, but accurate, cliche', one does not understand an idea fully until one can write about it. We do not believe that one can teach thinking the same way one can teach the multiplication tables, but it is clear that a student who is a good writer is generally perceived by his or her teachers as an effective thinker as well. Learning to write involves learning to think, and writing is unique in allowing students not only to think, but to display the products of their thinking in a form that invites further contemplation.

HOW TO USE THIS BOOK

This book is written with a very broad audience in mind. It is designed both for teachers who have previously taught writing but who want to move into content-writing topics and for teachers who are novices at teaching writing but who think it might be important to do with their students.

Part I, then, offers a primer for the writing teacher—novice or experienced—some basic principles and procedures that show all teachers just how easy it is to start content writing in their classes. Part II offers specific examples—model units and lessons—and some teachers may wish to turn directly to that section and examine the pedagogical principles later. Part III, concerned with applications and extensions, shows teachers how to move beyond the sample lessons to develop specific materials for their own classrooms.

Throughout the book, we have taken pains to show that teaching writing in the content areas is *not* an add-on, not just another burden for the busy teacher. Content writing can be integrated within the existing day, within the existing curriculum, enhancing instruction rather than becoming an independent component of it. Even theme evaluation, which is often perceived as a task so large as to discourage teachers from teaching writing, can be integrated naturally into the content teaching of a class.

This book also has another broad audience in mind, an indirect audience: the students of the teachers who will read it. We have taught writing in the content areas in inner-city schools, in a summer writing camp for youngsters from disadvantaged settings, in suburban schools, in afterschool young writers' workshops, and even to college students and faculty members. We have seen that it can energize previously uninspired writers—of whom there are a vast number in this country. Finally, then, we hope that the ideas and examples presented here will motivate the teachers who read them to join the ranks of those teachers who already see the enormous value and pleasure involved in teaching writing in the content areas.

Part I

A Primer on Teaching Writing in the Content Areas

You don't need a college degree in English to teach content-area writing. You don't have to be an expert in grammar or know how to diagram a sentence or be able to explain the difference between a direct and indirect object. You don't have to be a walking dictionary or thesaurus, and you don't have to be an expert on contemporary usage and style. You don't even need to feel you are an outstanding writer yourself (although that certainly wouldn't hurt). In short, you don't have to be trained as a specialist to teach interdisciplinary writing.

As a matter of fact, if you are *not* a specialist, you may have a distinct advantage: namely, that you don't have a preconceived notion about how writing "must" be taught. Too often the teaching of writing has been made overly complex by specialists, especially in teaching students complicated and abstract concepts of rhetoric and grammar. This primer keeps things simple, not because we underestimate your intelligence or experience, but because you can carry out content-area writing instruction successfully if you keep in mind just a few precepts and apply them consistently. As a matter of fact, one principle is central to our philosophy of content-area writing. From it, all else follows:

Keep content at the center of the writing process.

This principle gives *clarity of content* top priority. Students first need to know a subject well and then must be committed to presenting their thoughts clearly to an audience. Good writing follows from that formula. You probably know from your own experience the effect knowing the material can have on your writing. Can you recall going into an exam feeling shaky about your mastery of the subject? What happened to your writing? Did it become weak, tentative, evasive, or uncertain, betraying your limited grasp of the content? Was it different when you went to the exam with the material clearly in mind? Chances are it was then more confident, firm, and vigorous, even forceful and clear.

But good writing involves more than mere subject matter knowledge. Many adults know volumes but cannot write successfully. Sometimes that can be traced to a failure to focus knowledge, to take a stance or point of view toward it, or to phrase the material for a particular kind of reader. Too many school writing assignments use writing solely as a way to "prove" mastery of content by repeating what was learned in class and from texts. In such cases, students do not focus their writing or take a stand on the material. In contrast, a well-designed writing activity builds in stance and point of view and even provides an audience for writing to assist students in organizing their knowledge and in selecting a structure for it in writing.

Much of teaching writing in the content areas consists not in telling students *how* to write, but in creating situations where they want to write and want to write well, using their subject-matter knowlege in the process. The four steps discussed in the next few pages are those used in our own teaching and in developing the model content-area activities that appear in Part II.

A PROCEDURE FOR DEVELOPING CONTENT-AREA WRITING LESSONS

1. Determine content objectives. Whatever you are teaching, the first question to answer is: What do you want your students to learn? Content-area writing works best when it involves *discovery*, *synthesis*, and *inquiry* rather than recitation of factual material. Although teachers *can* use writing to have students merely list what they know on a subject, often a multiple-choice or short-answer test is more efficient and truer to the use of language for that purpose. Save the real writing assignments for the times when you want students to put their learning together and apply it to new situations.

As an illustration, suppose a teacher was doing a unit on the solar system. In a factually oriented class, the learning objectives might focus on such matters as knowing the names of the planets, their location in space relative to the sun, their characteristics, and, perhaps, the origins of their names in classical mythology. Such information—if it were the only aim of the unit—would be examined most easily through multiple-choice or short-answer tests.

A teacher interested in having students *synthesize* and *apply* their knowledge might have a broader set of objectives, such as helping students come to—

- Understand (or at least partially comprehend) the vastness of the solar system—to feel the distances, not just know them.
- Explore the possibilities for travel to the other planets (possibly as an antidote to the impressions created by popular television programs).
- Understand the various theories of the origins of our solar system and weigh the evidence supporting each theory.

Unit objectives would be rather broad, possibly creating the framework for several weeks' work. Presumably the teacher would also create more specific objectives for individual class lessons and/or writing activities.

In any event, the cardinal principle is that *content objectives should be established first*, prior to the writing activities.

2. Develop writing ideas to explore the objectives. Often teachers think of writing assignments in only two discourse modes— the essay and the report—and give them in barebones fashion, with few instructions to the writer:

> Write an essay or report on the origins of the solar system and explain the locations of the nine planets.

Sometimes the assignment specifies length as well:

> Your paper should be at least two pages (or ten pages or 500 words or 1,000 words in length).

Most of us have probably written papers on topics that were not spelled out in much more detail. Such assignments often fail because they do not explore the range of writing forms available to the student and they supply little assistance to the writer. By their very brevity they invite failure.

There are a number of ways to express content ideas in writing, and a good interdisciplinary writing program will explore many of them. The principal objectives of the solar system unit, for example, can be explored in several different modes of discourse, including the following:

> *Fiction*—"Write a short story about travel from one planet to another, with your hero or heroine telling about what he/she observes."

Journalism—"You are the editor of *Interplanetary Gazette*, a video newspaper that is circulated throughout the solar system. Write some news stories telling what life is like on each planet."

Media—"Suppose you were preparing a television special about the solar system. Write a plan for the program. What kinds of information and film shots would you want to include?"

The writing can, of course, be done in more conventional forms of school writing:

Essay—"What do you think about the possibilities for space travel in your lifetime? Write an essay in which you suggest just how common you think interplanetary travel will be by, say, the year 2050."

Report—"Rocketry has come a long way since World War II, when crude rockets were first used in warfare. Make a study of the major advancements in rocket design in the past forty years and write a report."

Figure 1 is a list of the different kinds of discourse forms that can easily be drawn upon for content-area assignments. In our own teaching we use this list and try to create a range of choices for students so that they are regularly encountering new ways to express their knowledge. The essential question for the teacher at this point is: How can students best get their ideas on the subject into writing? Sometimes the form of a *play* or a *story* will be best. At others, a letter written to another person may be a good option. Older students may find expository writing easier to do than some of the so-called creative writing forms, but creative writing of poems, plays, stories, songs is an appropriate way to express ideas at all levels.

Whenever possible, we offer our students a range of writing ideas with several different ways to satisfy the main assignment. We have already given five options on the solar system topic. But teachers can have students consider projects that go beyond spoken or written language into art and music:

Draw or paint your impressions of the planet Venus.

Or:

Find some classical music that fits your impressions of the planet Venus and play it for the class or to back up your drawing of what you think the planet looks like.

SOME DISCOURSE FORMS FOR CONTENT WRITING

Journals and diaries
  (real or imaginary)
Biographical sketches
Anecdotes and stories:
  from experience
  as told by others
Thumbnail sketches:
  of famous people
  of places
  of content ideas
  of historical events
Guess who/what descriptions
Letters:
  personal reactions
  observations
  public/informational
  persuasive:
    to the editor
    to public officials
  to imaginary people
  from imaginary places
Requests
Applications
Memos
Resume's and summaries
Poems
Plays
Stories
Fantasy
Adventure
Science fiction
Historical stories
Dialogues and conversations
Children's books
Telegrams
Editorials
Commentaries
Responses and rebuttals
Newspaper "fillers"
Fact books or fact sheets
School newspaper stories
Stories or essays for local papers
Proposals
Case studies:
  school problems
  local issues
  national concerns
  historical problems
  scientific issues
Songs and ballads
Demonstrations
Poster displays

Reviews:
  books (including textbooks)
  films
  outside reading
  television programs
  documentaries
Historical "you are there" scenes
Scence notes:
  observations
  science notebook
  reading reports
  lab reports
Math:
  story problems
  solutions to problems
  record books
  notes and observations
Responses to literature
Utopian proposals
Practical proposals
Interviews:
  actual
  imaginary
Directions:
  how-to
  school or neighborhood guide
  survival manual
Dictionaries and lexicons
Technical reports
Future options, notes on:
  careers, employment
  school and training
  military/public service
Written debates
Taking a stand:
  school issues
  family problems
  state or national issues
  moral questions
Books and booklets
Informational monographs
Radio scripts
TV scenarios and scripts
Dramatic scripts
Notes for improvised drama
Cartoons and cartoon strips
Slide show scripts
Puzzles and word searches
Prophecy and predictions
Photos and captions
Collage, montage, mobile,
  sculpture

FIGURE 1

While these latter projects are not the heart of a *writing* program, they suggest yet another interdisciplinary connection and use some of the essential processes of writing, including finding an idea, locating information, organizing the information for an audience, and presenting it.

Finally, we like to give our students one additional choice:

> If none of the ideas I've given you about writing about the solar system appeals to you, make up your own idea. Just check with me before you begin to write.

The more students write, the more likely they are to have developed their imaginations and the more likely they are to choose that open-ended topic, in essence, inventing their own assignments. So much the better, we think.

As part of our writing projects, we also try to build in an audience for student writers. Including provisions for an audience in an assignment helps students write for someone other than the teacher and adds a strong element of reality to the writing process. The audience for writing can be an imaginary one—especially for younger writers:

> After months of travel through outer space, you have landed your craft on Mars. Once you have stretched your legs and gotten use to the lower gravity, you decide to send a Space-O-Gram back to your earthbound family. What do you tell them about what you have seen?

Sometimes the audience becomes the other students, who can be invited to join in the fantasy and role play the audience or even write back from the point of view of that audience:

> Your parent has just sent you a Space-O-Gram from Mars describing life on that planet. What additional questions do you have? Write a Space-O-Gram back requesting more information.

Often, however, the audiences for student writing can be real, giving writers a sense that their writing can be helpful in the real world:

> Write to the National Aeronautics and Space Administration in Washington, D.C., requesting information on NASA's future plans for interplanetary space travel.

13

Other audiences for student writing can range from the class to other students in the school to administrators to parents to public officials (at the state or local level) to nationally famous people. Whenever feasible, then, add focus to writing activities by specifying the real or imaginary audience for them.

A good composition assignment or activity not only needs to be explicit, it should also make clear to students precisely what they must do to complete the assignment successfully. For example, inexperienced writers almost invariably want to know something about length—"How long does it have to be?"—a habit often learned in classes where teachers had them write to specific word lengths— 500 or 1,000. Instead of turning students into word counters, help them understand how long a composition should be in terms of its intrinsic need to satisfy the assignment. The appropriate length of a piece of writing is *long enough to get the job done*, but teachers can supply some hints:

> Write up an interview between the astronaut who has just returned from the moon and a reporter for the evening news. Think of five or six good questions for the interviewer to ask and then write the astronaut's answers.

Or:

> Have your astronaut write a summary of his/her observations about the possibility of life on planet Mars for the Director of NASA. The Director is a busy person, so make the summary as concise as possible, but don't leave out any important details.

The assignments should also make clear the purpose of the writing (especially if students are writing an examination). Students should know from the teacher's oral or written comments just why this writing is being done:

> To show that you understand how our solar system works, write as if you were a comet, just entering the system and heading toward the sun, describing what you see.

It is also important for the oral or written assignment to include some guidance to get students started finding any material they need to complete it successfully. This might be as simple as reading a chapter in the textbook:

> After you have read the chapter on planets in your text,

pick one planet and write a brief description of it in your journal.

More often (and more imaginatively) the assignment can suggest sources of ideas beyond the classroom:

The Astronomers' Club invites guests to its meetings. If you think you'd like to attend one, let me know and we'll make arrangements. That way you'll have some firsthand information for use in your solar system paper.

Or:

Go to the library and get a biography of Galileo. After you've read it, either write a description of the solar system as he imagined it, or pretend you are Galileo and write a letter to a friend describing all the difficulties you are having persuading people to accept your view of the solar system.

No single written assignment can fully teach writing or prepare students to engage with complete success in the writing process. But we hope this section has helped teachers see the range of content-area writing possibilities that exists, as well as the importance of careful design and **planning** of the assignment for a successful student writing experience.

3. Teach writing and learning. Once the assignment is made, the real content teaching begins, but as we emphasized earlier, *teaching content is also teaching writing.* This can be divided into several stages: *prewriting, writing, revising, copyediting,* and *presenting and publishing.*

Prewriting. Before students put pen to paper, their preparation is very important. This is the time when they either master their basic content or fail to understand it, with predictable results in their writing. Although teachers at the upper levels may want to assign an impromptu theme from time to time as preparation for examination writing, the impromptu, with its focus on instant writing, is generally a poor form for practice; it is something only advanced writers can do successfully. We urge teachers to spend a great deal of time at the prewriting/learning stage—an hour, a day, sometimes a week or more—helping students gather information and prepare to write. Good content teaching enters at this point as students read, discuss, and think about their material.

Here are some ways the teacher can focus the prewriting stage:

■ Have students keep logs or notebooks or journals of their learning. These should contain basic notes or ideas, of course, but more important, they should provide students with an avenue to respond in personal terms to what they are learning. They can write about their puzzlements, amazements, astounding and interesting facts, and things "I never knew before." Journals of this sort are usually left ungraded, simply checked from time to time by the teacher for their informational content.

■ Provide prewriting discussions of the topic and assignment. Sometimes this can be done in small groups; at others, through teacher-led discussion. In the discussion students can talk over questions about the assignment, where they can find information, the audience for the writing, the range of choices and options available.

■ Encourage students to develop their own set of planning strategies. *Don't require formal outlines for papers.* Instead, urge students to make plans, in writing, according to a pattern that feels comfortable to them. Some people like to make long, elaborate sets of notes before writing, others prefer to jot down just a few words. Still others like to go through their notebooks or journals, circling the important ideas and numbering them in order, finally jotting down a plan for writing as a final journal entry. Every writer needs to do some planning before writing, but the conventional outline inhibits more student writers than it helps.

Such written planning, even if done on scratch paper, helps the teacher ensure that the student has, in fact, mastered or understood the content material. If students cannot plan, jot down some notes or ideas on paper, the teacher has a clue that more prewriting is necessary.

■ Have students talk through their papers with the teacher or another student before writing. This oral strategy is extremely helpful in clarifying the thoughts and ideas of young writers before they commit themselves to writing. It need not take long—perhaps five or ten minutes—and it invariably produces good results in terms of the clarity and focus of the writing.

Writing. Many teachers think of the writing stage as a time to sit back and relax, a time to wait before the onslaught of another batch of papers for grading. But *as* students write, teachers can do much to help raise the quality of their writing and learning.

When students are writing during class time, the teacher can take an active role. For example, monitor facial expressions—they often tell when a student is starting to get in a jam and needs help. Float about the class during a writing assignment, glancing at first paragraphs and rough beginnings, offering advice if it seems needed and respecting students' need to be left alone if your presence makes them nervous. In other words, help students get it right *while* they are writing and encourage them to solve their problems the first time around. This helps cut down on the amount of revision needed later.

Also encourage students to talk to one another during the writing process—unless, of course, the writing is an examination of some sort. There are great benefits from such forms of peer collaboration as encouraging writers to bounce ideas off one another, reading draft paragraphs aloud to seek advice, pumping their friends for new ideas. As long as this collaboration occurs publicly and within the spirit of fair play, there is no danger of students cheating or turning in something that is not their own.

Other ideas for teaching during the writing process:

■ Tell students not to worry about spelling, punctuation, and mechanics at the rough draft stage. If their concerns about correctness inhibit them from writing, however, encourage them to ask questions about correctness as items or problems come up. Be sure not to attach any penalties or embarrassment to such requests for help.

■ Provide assistance for students who get stuck with a writing block. Nine times out of ten such a block comes from a content failure: the writer just does not know what to say about the topic. But other problems can lead writers to freeze while writing. If students cannot get the opening paragraph down on paper, suggest that they write the second paragraph first and not worry about the beginning until later. Sometimes a little free association will help unclog a pen. Some writers even write the *end* of their papers before going back to write the earlier parts. Conversation is also an unblocker, and the teacher can help out by simply saying, "Tell me what it is you want to write about." Once the student has told about his or her plan, the teacher can say, "You've just done it. Now all you have to do is write it down."

■ Provide as much support as possible through the content matter of the writing. Help students focus on what they know and the audience with whom they will be sharing their knowledge. That kind of focus will bring clarity to their writing.

■ Create the tone of a collaborative workshop in the class. Don't let the room be a silent tomb where everyone works at writing in isolation.

It is probably obvious that we generally favor in-class to out-of-class writing. When students are writing on school time, teachers can control the process much more successfully. However, even if students write at home, teachers can monitor their progress. For example, teachers can urge students to keep in touch as they write and to give them daily progress reports on papers being written outside class. If a student has some writing problems and cannot solve them, it is better to hear about them before the day the paper is due.

Revising. Research in writing shows that astonishingly few young writers—elementary, secondary, even college level—know much about revising a paper. To many students, "revise" simply means, "Make a clean copy in your best handwriting." However, as numerous professional writers have reported, good writing usually means good *re*writing. Drafts are often rough and inaccurate, representing a struggle to get words down on the page. Rewriting brings focus and clarity. It is important that teachers encourage revision as a part of every paper they assign.

It is also important to distinguish between *revising* and *copyediting*. The latter has to do with the surface correctness of the manuscript, and it should occur at the end of the writing process. *Revising* means working with the content of a paper—moving ideas around, adding needed information, taking out redundant material.

Revising can often be a community activity, with students serving successfully as their own editors, commenting on their papers and making suggestions for changes. To initiate a group revision session, divide the class into threes or fours or fives, either self-selected or teacher-assigned groups. Then have students share papers— sometimes with the author reading the draft of his/her paper aloud to the group, sometimes with papers passed around for written comments and responses. Caution students that this is not a red-penciling session for nitpicking about spelling and grammar. Nor is it an opportunity for cutting down their neighbors. Rather, it is a way for writers to get some sense of how their papers affect a small group of readers. It is the single best way we know of to help writers see the kinds of changes they need to make.

Small group revising of papers also helps solve a problem that may be the biggest barrier to teachers' doing more content-area writing: the theme-correcting burden. Many teachers we have met say they would like to do more writing in their classes, but they do not have time to correct all the papers students produce. To such teachers we recommend peer revising. It reduces theme grading to a reasonable level in several ways:

1. It places the responsibility for revision with the proper person—the *writer*.
2. The group work involved creates flexible time for the teacher to use for individual conferences, providing concrete help on a

face-to-face basis that is far more efficient than writing comments on themes.

3. The papers turned in are better than those that are simply dashed off in class and given to the teacher to read. Many teachers who use group revision report theme reading to be a pleasure, not a chore, consisting primarily of logging in good, successful papers rather than penning critical comments on a batch of rough drafts.

Of course, the teacher cannot be passive in peer revising sessions— they are not successful by magic. The teacher needs to structure them carefully so that students know what is expected and precisely how to go about revising one another's work. To begin such a session, review the assignment with the class, reminding students what was expected, for whom the paper was written, the kind of content it was to contain, and so on. Then have students respond to the paper in terms of the content that it presents. Is it clear? Does it make sense? Can other students understand it? Could outsiders understand it? What changes would help? A good way to organize these sessions is to provide the class with a sheet with a few focus questions for the day as shown in Figure 2. A longer list of questions for teachers to use to make their own revising sheets appears in Figure 3. Naturally, the complexity of these question can be adjusted to match the skills of students.

SAMPLE REVISING SHEET

Today I want you to focus on whether or not the writer kept the audience in mind during the writing process. Answer these questions in your small groups.

1. Who is the best audience for this paper as it is written? Can you describe the people who would be most interested in it?

2. Did the writer tell the audience everything it needs to know to understand the topic? Help the writer figure out if anything is left out.

3. Did the writer perhaps tell too much? Is there more information here than an audience can possibly handle? Help the writer figure out where to cut.

4. After you have completed your small group discussion, write a note to the author, reacting to the paper as if you were a member of the audience.

FIGURE 2

OTHER QUESTIONS FOR REVISING GROUPS

Note: Do not have students ask *all* these questions (or similar ones) at every revising session. Rather, pick some questions that seem most appropriate to your assignment and have the students work on two or three each time.

PURPOSE
- Where is this writing headed? Can readers clearly tell?
- Is it on one track, or does it shoot off in new directions?
- Is the writer trying to do too much? Too little?
- Does the author seem to *care* about his her/writing?

CONTENT
- When you're through, can you easily summarize this piece or retell it in your own words?
- Can a reader understand it easily?
- Are there parts that you found confusing?
- Are there parts that need more explanation or evidence?
- Are there places where the writer said too much, or overexplained the subject?
- Can the reader visualize the subject?
- Does it hold your interest all the way through?
- Did you learn something new from this paper?

ORGANIZATION
- Do the main points seem to be in the right order?
- Does the writer give you enough information so that you know what he/she is trying to accomplish?
- Does the writing begin smoothly? Does the writer take too long to get started?
- What about the ending? Does it end crisply and excitingly?

AUDIENCE
- Who are the readers for this writing? Does the writer seem to have them clearly in mind? Will they understand him/her?
- Does the writer assume too much from the audience? Too little?
- What changes does the writer need to make to better communicate with the audience?

LANGUAGE AND STYLE
- Is the paper interesting and readable? Does it get stuffy or dull?
- Can you hear the writer's voice and personality in it?
- Are all difficult words explained or defined?
- Does the writer use natural, lively language throughout?
- Are the grammar, spelling, and punctuation OK?

FIGURE 3

Not all teachers are comfortable with peer revision of papers. There can be some problems: students do not always give one another good advice; sometimes group members do not have rapport; and sometimes students give each other bland approval instead of needed criticism. Nevertheless, we strongly urge teachers to try peer revising more than once—don't just try it once and give it up if it doesn't seem to work right away. This method helps students learn to become responsible for the quality of their own work, and in that respect, it is one of the most important skills a young writer can master.

Copyediting. It is extremely important that teachers not introduce concerns for spelling, punctuation, and mechanics too early in the writing process. And it is important that students learn how to get their final copies into standard edited English. But such concerns should not take priority over matters of content.

Now is the time for teacher and students to be concerned with correctness, after the paper has been planned and organized and shaped and drafted and revised. Now is the time for the teacher to have students work on spelling problems and usage errors, guiding them to the correct forms. We believe it is crucial for the teacher to train students to take responsibility for the final correctness of their work. The teacher should not be a copyeditor.

A great deal has been written in recent years about the appropriateness of compelling all students, especially those who are members of racial and ethnic minorities, to write in a uniform standard English. In general, composition researchers have come to feel that it is inappropriate to try to eradicate the dialect of a student's upbringing, and, further, that dwelling on matters of correctness seldom teaches "good English" and often inhibits students from writing well. At the same time, there is a "real world," a world that penalizes and even ridicules those who do not adhere to the conventions of standard written English.

We suggest that the concern for correctness be introduced very gradually, and that at no time a student be made to feel that the dialect he or she uses quite comfortably at home and with peers is somehow inadequate or second-rate. Most dialects, in fact, are both sophisticated and appropriate for the situations in which they are used. The best route to correctness is through publishing student writing, a topic to be discussed next. Further, small group work is again helpful in giving students an awareness that the conventions of standard written English are not just arbitrary—they help people communicate more successfully. In a group of four or five students,

21

most major misspellings and usage errors can be identified, even with very young writers. The copyediting sessions will not always produce perfect papers, but they will help students learn how to go about this final stage of the process. We are confident that teachers who try group copyediting for a semester or a year will be happy with the results, and will see students grow in their ability to check their own papers.

However, teachers who are not satisfied with the results of these sessions can follow up with written comments and suggestions on the papers. We do *not* recommend marking every error on every paper, a chore that is time-consuming for the teacher and disheartening for the student. Rather, we suggest picking one or two errors that seem to come up regularly in the student's work and concentrating on those.

Above all, don't give student writers the impression that correctness is the be-all and end-all of writing. Keep the focus and the praise on *content*, and work on mechanics gradually, as a peripheral matter.

Presenting and publishing. Writing that is done solely for the teacher, or solely for a grade, is often not highly motivated. To motivate students to do their best writing, include provision for presentation and publication whenever possible. This can be as simple as posting papers on a bulletin board or having them read aloud to the class; or publishing class newspapers and magazines, using ditto or mimeograph to produce something students can take home and share. Pat Edwards, a teacher in New South Wales, Australia, has compiled a list of 101 different ways to publish student writing,[5] including the following:

- Books (individual books, collaborative books, textbooks written for the whole class)
- Newspapers (school news, family news, natural science reports)
- Magazines (on almost any conceivable subject matter topic)
- Plays (as a way of presenting written ideas for an audience)
- Letters (sent within the class through a postal system or letters actually mailed)
- Bulletin boards and display centers
- School assemblies (for presenting work orally, often with audiovisual aids)
- Storefront displays (getting student writing out into the community)
- Tape recording (to create an oral library of writing).

Publishing writing provides an incentive for students to do a good job of revising and copyediting, but more significantly, it shows them that writing is important because it brings them a readership and a response or reaction. It is the payoff to the writing process.

4. Followup. Too often writing assignments seem to be made in isolation, as one-time-only events unrelated to the rest of the class and its activities. When writing in the content areas is well taught, it provides natural possibilities for additional work. One writing idea leads to another: a piece of fantasy writing becomes the starting point for a series of stories; a kitchen science experiment with electricity suggests ideas for a booklet on similar experiments. Other areas of a topic can be explored through writing, leading to a classroom where students have a piece of content writing in the works at all times. Even the presentation stage of writing can lead to followup activities, as one piece of student writing generates a response from students that encourages them to start off on a new writing project. Writing leads to writing, as the model lessons that follow demonstrate.

LESSON FORM FOR CONTENT-AREA WRITING ACTIVITIES

1. Determine content objectives.

2. Develop writing ideas that explore the content concepts.

3. Teach writing and learning:
   A. Prewriting
   B. Writing
   C. Revising
   D. Copyediting
   E. Presenting and Publishing

4. Followup

FIGURE 4

Part II

Model Units for Teaching Writing in the Content Areas

Teachers can study the units that follow in one of two ways: (1) they can read them and glean the principles of interdisciplinary teaching from them before designing their own lessons, or (2) they can test some of the lessons in their own classes. We think the second option is preferable in that teaching, like writing, is a learn-by-doing skill. The comments and suggestions will probably make more sense if the ideas are tested in the classroom. In this case, it will be helpful to know that each unit is designed to stand independently of others, and none requires any previous experience teaching writing in the content areas.

The units vary in length. Some can be completed in a day or two; others may require a week. Drawing on the suggested followup activities, some can be extended to a month or a year. Teachers should not feel it is necessary to make their content lessons as complete and lengthy as the ones described here—they can whittle them down to the size that fits their own class. Further, these are lesson ideas, not blueprints. Many alternative ideas and teaching strategies have been included so that units can be adapted to the needs of students.

IN OUR TIME

To many students, "history" is either a dull textbook to be carried home and studied or a collection of legendary stories about heroes and heroines, crises and resolutions. To help students understand more fully that history is something alive, something in the process of becoming, this unit has them assemble a scrapbook that reflects their knowledge and thinking about the world.

Content Objectives

■ To have students analyze and describe the present in terms of its history-making potential.

■ To encourage students to take a lively interest in current events.

■ To learn about ways of augmenting knowledge through outside reading and informal research.

Writing Ideas

This unit offers students a wide range of writing options. Each piece of writing is to be contributed to the class scrapbook entitled *In Our Time.*

■ Write a "Dear Abby" letter and a response discussing what you see as an important social concern of our time, for example, *dating, marriage, divorce, adoption, parent/child relationships, peer relationships, school, drugs, work.*

■ Write a review for the local or school paper of a newly released book or film that you have just read or seen and comment on the ways you think it reflects values in today's society. (Make a carbon of your review to include in the scrapbook.)

■ Write a diary, fictional or real, about happenings in the typical high school student's life. Entries can treat changes occurring in the family, school, or community; typical thoughts about the world; the kinds of pressures and responsibilities that come with growing up and entering the adult world. Add the entries that you are willing to share to the class scrapbook.

■ Write a free association essay or poem about education today.

■ Write an editorial to the local or school paper taking a firm stand on a local issue that is important to you. (Save the carbon for the scrapbook.)

■ Take a series of photographs that represent to you the characteristics of life in our time, in our town. Then write a short paragraph for each photograph explaining what you believe it represents. (You may want to leave blank pages following your comments for others to add their ideas. Are your classmates' interpretations of your photographs different from yours?)

■ Write a letter to a local politician or to a state or federal legislator expressing your views on a topic of current concern. (Save a carbon. Also include the politician's reply in the scrapbook.)

■ List ten recent events that you think might change the world, your community, or your school in some substantial way. Then write a commentary explaining your views on each event.

■ Study new directions in one of the following fields and write about how they may reshape history: *medicine, law, science, government, education, technology.*

■ List ten people who may be shaping history in your school, community, state, nation, or the world. Then write a feature article about the person you know most about or are most interested in. Supplement your knowledge with recent magazine and newspaper articles or with personal interviews.

■ Write a column similar to that of Art Buchwald or Erma Bombeck commenting humorously on current events.

■ Write a song lyric (and possibly the music) for a composition reflecting current concerns or lifestyles in the 1980s.

■ Write a prophecy about important world happenings during the next twenty years. Make two copies: one for the class scrapbook, one to save for yourself to read after the turn of the century.

Writing and Learning

Prewriting

To complete the project, students will need to have the following material available:

■ Current newspapers and magazines such as *Science Digest, Time, Newsweek, Harpers, The Atlantic, Saturday Review, Scientific American, National Geographic, Psychology Today, Nation's Business*

■ A separate notebook for notes and drafts

■ Posterboard for display and heavy art paper for the scrapbook

■ Cameras and film for pictorial essays.

Each student can probably carry out several of the assignments listed, depending on the time allowed for the project. For each activity, students will need to do some preliminary planning, reading, notetaking, and eventually drafting of ideas. They can plan and write at home or in class. The teacher may wish to spot-check their notebooks once a week or set aside part of a class period two or three times a week to help those who are having difficulties and to establish a regular writing routine.

The notebook is a good place for students to summarize articles on recent events or to review television news. Their note-taking should be informal, limited to a few articles, and consisting of pertinent facts and details. Also encourage students to respond and react to their reading, not to content themselves with simply jotting down the cold, hard facts.

After students have completed one or two assignments from the list, the teacher may wish to encourage the class to develop additional assignments. Often a student's reading and related study will naturally suggest further directions and resources to follow. In this way the unit builds and students become even more actively engaged in seeing how history is made.

Writing, Revising, Copyediting

In this project, drafting is a rather continuous process, with students writing whenever they have completed some research on a topic. Thirty students may be working on thirty very different topics, each proceeding at his/her own pace. This kind of individualized writing provides an ideal opportunity for the teacher to coach students through the drafting stage, offering help to those who need it.

From time to time, as drafts are completed, set aside a class period for peer reading and response. Have students exchange drafts, working in small groups to evaluate how well the ideas are developed, whether or not they are clear and the presentation interesting. For example, students can point out what they find most interesting in a draft, underline what they think is the main idea, ask questions about areas that pique their curiosity, and indicate places where they lost track of the ideas or the main thrust of a paper. This procedure will help writers see where to add details, where to cut or add sections, how to reorganize or find ways to make their writing clear.

Then comes copyediting. The teacher can appoint the spelling, grammar, and punctuation whizzes in class to answer questions or help other students copyedit. At the same time, the teacher can spot-check drafts and answer questions. Or write the common spelling, grammar, or punctuation problems on the board and have students look for them in their own or each other's papers.

Presentation and Publication

Before students copy materials into the scrapbook, the teacher should collect the work and evaluate it. This can include pointing out any errors students have missed, although the copy should be reasonably clean if they have followed the previous stages. Then students can prepare a final copy of their various contributions and, as a class, plan how to organize the selections in the scrapbook. The work can be mounted on large sheets of heavy art or construction paper and the pages punched and held together with notebook rings. A class member should also do a cover and prepare illustrations.

The big question for students to answer is, "How do we organize the book?" In organizing the material, they will be making their own historical assessment of what is important in their time. Help them think of alternative ways to do this—following a local/state/ national pattern, an "issues" plan, a chronological sequence.

At this point, it would also be useful for several students to write introductory matter for the scrapbook. This can include an overall description of the plan of the book, as well as introductions for individual sections. Although just a few students will write these materials, the entire class should contribute to the planning, perhaps even to the extent of making a chalkboard outline for each writer to follow.

The final product, the scrapbook, should be available for contributors and other students to browse through and read at their leisure. Then it can become a part of a bulletin board display, and eventually perhaps go to the library as a reference. If the project is repeated year after year, the library will soon have a fascinating collection of scrapbooks and an impressive record of recent history.

Followup

The journal writing assignments suggested earlier lend themselves quite naturally to a number of spinoff projects:

■ Compile a book of etiquette for the 1980s that discusses social conventions, dress codes, and language of students your age.

■ Write a chapter for a social science, science, or history book to be read 20, 50, or 100 years hence describing today's happenings.

■ Review the quality of treatment of current events in a range of popular magazines. What different views about an issue do you find from reading, say, *Time* and *The Atlantic,* or *Science Digest* and *Scientific American*?

■ Write a television script or drama that reflects the life of a teenager in today's world. Rehearse and present your play.

SCIENCE AND YOUR LIFE

Like language, science touches virtually everything we perceive or do. Science is not just a satellite circling the earth; it help us understand such everyday things as why it is necessary to keep rice covered while it is cooking. This unit asks students to draw on the knowledge they already have about science and apply it to the world as it exists and as it may exist in the future. By developing their ideas and insights and sharing them with others, students can see how effective applications of science can improve the quality of life for all people.

Content Objectives

■ To have students make their own discoveries and hypotheses, synthesizing scientific information with their knowledge of the present.
■ To encourage students to use their knowledge of science and present-day life to make predictions about the future.
■ To teach students basic and applied research skills.

Writing Ideas

This unit offers students five possible projects to complete in physics, chemistry, or general science courses, leading to varied modes of presentation:

■ From the recent data on the chemical and climatic conditions on Mars, Jupiter, or Venus, consider what possible life forms could exist on those planets or how humankind might adapt itself to live on them. Write (and perhaps illustrate) a scenario showing life on other planets.
■ Look at some of the newest materials being fabricated (metal compounds such as Nitonol or powered metals, some of the wonder fabrics made from petroleum products) and devise new uses for them. Write a report for members of the general public who understand little about such new products.
■ Think about the "free" energy sources available to us (such as wind, sun, rain, ocean and river currents, garbage, melting snow and icebergs, gravity, geothermal activity) and devise systems for using

one of these sources. Write a proposal to the local, state, or federal government for the use of one of these energy sources.

■ Make a list of things which currently exist but which you predict or fear may disappear in the future. For example, what do you think will become of the gasoline-powered car, of trains, telephones, zoos, typewriters, weather forecasters, electric can openers, and so on? Select an item you think may disappear or be radically altered and describe its future.

■ Invent something new. What is one thing you think the world needs? Plan and write a prospectus or idea sheet for your invention.

If these five assignments are longer than time or course allows, substitute some of the following, shorter projects:

■ List ten or more predictions about what will happen in the major scientific fields during the next 50 or 100 years. Jot down anything that occurs to you; then go through your list, pick one prediction, and study its feasibility.

■ Write a short article to include in a newspaper or popular scientific magazine in the year 2025. What new invention or scientific discovery will be making news 50 years from now?

■ Conduct an oral or written debate on a current scientific issue: cloning, life on Mars, nuclear power, extinction of species, DNA duplication and genetic engineering, robots, automobile pollution.

■ Write and deliver a simulated news broadcast covering a human landing on another planet.

■ List the five or ten scientific discoveries that have affected your life most strongly. Select one to learn more about and find out what led to its discovery.

Writing and Learning

Prewriting

Although described as appropriate for science classes, this unit involves a good deal of English-type research—reading and note-taking. Thus students will need access to local or school libraries to read about most of the topics. They may also be able to contact local businesses or industries or specific people in the community for information. All students should keep a notebook to record observations, to develop their ideas and hypotheses, and to complete the prewriting stages of their projects.

To guide students in their research, prepare a probe sheet (see Figure 5). This will lead them not only to written sources, but to community members, businesspeople, and the media.

PROBE SHEET

Use the following questions to guide you in planning your research. Write down ideas, answers, titles, etc. in your notebook.

1. Look through the list of class projects and list several that interest you. Then narrow your topic to your first choice, or propose an alternative topic if you have a better idea.

2. Describe in broad outline what you already know about your subject. Where did you learn this information? Are you certain it is correct?

3. What don't you know? List your unanswered questions. What do you need to know more about to complete your study successfully? Try to center your research on two or three central research questions.

4. Search for resources. Check the following for possible information:

    Magazines (check the serial holdings to find titles in your library)
    Books (look through the card catalog)
    Reports and Bulletins (ask the librarian to show you the pamphlet files)
    Other print resources

    People:
      Engineers
      Scientists
      Researchers
      Technicians
      Medical authorities
      University faculty
      Others

    Media Resources:
      Films (check through the library or through businesses and industry)
      Photographs (look for the library's photofile)
      Special reports and documentaries
      Others

FIGURE 5

For ideas on how scientists view the future, students can look at works by Arthur C. Clarke, Isaac Asimov, Carl Sagan, and other science/science fiction writers. They can examine science magazines like *Science Digest* and *Scientific American*. Most students live close enough to colleges and universities or to businesses and industries so that they can contact engineers and scientists and others connected with scientific exploration to fill in gaps in their knowledge.

As their notebooks grow larger, students will soon be ready to begin writing. At this point, a second handout, a project planning sheet, will guide them in getting started (see Figure 6).

PROJECT PLANNING SHEET

1. What is your subject and to what audience do you want to present your ideas? Who needs to know about this topic—your classmates? other students? your parents? the community?

2. What do you want to show or prove to your audience? What impact do you want to have on them?

3. List the basic ideas or points that are crucial to your audience's understanding of your project and purpose.

4. Choose a form of presentation for your project that lends itself to the audience and topic you have chosen:

   Oral presentation (with or without   Science fiction story
     visual illustrations)   Radio or TV drama
   Technical report (with or without   Poster display
     diagrams)   Case study report
   How-to article   Model of an invention
   Imaginary journal entries from   Imaginary radio interviews
     a scientist   Slide show
   Other: _____

5. Keeping in mind your answers to questions 1–4, describe how you can best present your ideas. Write a rough plan for your project (not necessarily in outline form). Talk with several classmates and collect their ideas too.

6. Write your rough draft, keeping in mind your audience and purpose. From time to time have somebody read over what you have written, even if it is in very rough form. Collect people's ideas and suggestions before you have gone too far to make changes.

FIGURE 6

Writing and Revising

The planning sheet carries students directly into the drafting phase. Once they have completed their drafts, they should split into small groups to discuss their first attempts, both the drafts of short stories and the notes for oral presentations. In the groups students can raise such questions as the following:

■ What seems most successful about this project so far? What do you like about it?

- What is the main point of the project? Is it easy to figure out?
- Is there any point where you became confused or lost interest? What does the writer need to do to hold your interest?
- Think about what you learned. Do you have any further questions?
- What is the best advice you can give the writer about how to make his/her presentation more successful?

After the initial revising session, the teacher can spend a class period or two helping students revise and rewrite their work, drawing on the small group suggestions. At this point students may need to do a bit more research, especially if their small groups raised questions they cannot easily answer.

As the drafts near completion, have students read their work aloud to listen for confusing sentences and catch copyreading errors. Do any sentences seem too long? Do some "float" on the page and seem not to connect with anything else? Are some sentences too short? This sort of oral reading is perhaps the single best self-revising technique students can use. Careful oral reading will enable writers to spot many kinds of problems that a silent reading will not reveal.

Presentation and Publication

If students are to share their findings with the class, they can publish some of their articles in a mimeographed class monograph or news sheet. Alternatively, they can make a one-of-a-kind display case presentation. The oral or dramatic presentations deserve showing to the whole class and possibly to other classes. If the audience for a project is broader than the school, the teacher can help students reach such audiences—writing to scientists, sending letters to the editor, preparing a project for the youth talent fair or local science fair.

Followup

Science is such a broad topic that it leads to innumerable writing-related projects. Among those we have either used with high school students or seen in use are the following:

- Write to the National Science Foundation about special summer science programs for high school students. In addition, the National Science Teachers Association (1742 Connecticut Ave., NW, Washington, DC 20009) can provide information regarding special science programs and opportunities for high schoolers.

■ Write to the Center for Innovation (Butte, Montana 59701) to find out how to market a new invention with a commercial company.

■ Start a science writers' club that is interested in exploring the future. Invite community members to join as well. Have interested people prepare papers on new scientific developments.

■ Organize a school-wide science fair featuring science writing.

■ Start a science fiction or science fact magazine in the school.

■ Start a Believe-It-Or-Not fact sheet about strange-but-true scientific phenomena.

■ Prepare radio programs on new scientific developments for possible broadcasting over a local station or playing over the school's public address system.

FAMILY HISTORY

Alex Haley's *Roots* helped Americans discover how knowledge of their origins often helps people understand their view of the world. This, of course, is a traditional goal of teaching history and social sciences. In recent years, many teachers have conducted "Roots" units, and many others know the value of the "Foxfire" approach to community cultural history developed by a Georgia English teacher, Eliot Wigginton. Such research also helps students see connections between themselves and the past—making historical dates, facts, names, and places come alive. This unit is designed to help students see their own place in history by examining their ancestry in relation to past events in the rest of the world.

Content Objectives

■ To provide students with an introduction to historical research methods.

■ To give students insights into their ancestry and the place they and their families have in history.

■ To provide correlations between North and South American history or other national or world histories that students are examining.

Writing Ideas

The long-range project for this unit is writing and assembling a *Family History Book* in which students collect memorabilia from relatives, interview family members about their experiences and recollections, and create a family tree. These data, however, can also be used as the starting point for some shorter assignments and spinoffs, including:

■ Short stories about periods of history

■ Imaginary journal entries or letters collected for a "Class of '23" (or any other year) notebook

■ Newspaper articles for an imaginary paper in a particular era

■ Passages from a history book incorporating the memories of people who have been interviewed

■ Scripts for radio broadcasts of "You Are There" programs: moments in family/U.S. history

■ Biographical sketches of family characters for a "Who's Who"
■ Selections for an etiquette or social manners book for a historical era.

The final projects can take the form of a scrapbook containing student writing, notes, and letters from family members; photographs, news clippings, and transcriptions of interviews with relatives. Alternatively, such projects might lead to—

■ A posterboard display depicting a family tree and including photographs, memorabilia, transcribed narratives, and commentaries.
■ An oral report incorporating narratives, photographs, memorabilia, and commentaries.
■ A taped history including relatives' voices about their recollections, as well as dramatic readings of clippings and family letters.

Writing and Learning

Prewriting

To prepare for the project, stock the classroom with several books on genealogical research such as *Your Family History* (Allan J. Lichtman, Vintage), *Finding Your Roots* (Jean Eddy Westin, Ballantine) and *Underfoot: An Everyday Guide to Exploring the American Past* (David Weitzman, Scribner's). These volumes will provide samples of cultural history research techniques. In addition, bring in or place on reserve some books on U.S. history covering basic periods going back at least to the Civil War. (The librarian or media specialist may also be able to locate audiovisual materials on the same periods to supplement the classroom collection.)

Begin the project by having students fill out the Roots Questionnaires and genealogical chart shown in Figures 7, 8, and 9. Of course, not all students come from families with a full complement of parents, grandparents, uncles, aunts, and cousins. For those who come from nontraditional families or for whom family data is not readily available, an alternative project might be suggested:

■ Write your autobiography (or several chapters of it), tracing and documenting your life so far.
■ Write a description of the world and our town on the day you were born.
■ Do a genealogy of the school, tracing its history as far back as you can, including the history of the building, its faculty, and students.

ROOTS QUESTIONNAIRE-1

Instructions: Ask your parents and other relatives to help you obtain as much information as possible about your ancestors. Don't worry if there are any gaps in the information. Also, ask for photographs of these people.

Information About Your Mother's Side of the Family

YOUR MOTHER

Maiden (unmarried) name: _____

Born (date): _____Place: _____

Names of her brothers and sisters (your uncles and aunts):

_____

YOUR MOTHER'S MOTHER (Your maternal grandmother)

Maiden name: _____

Born (date): _____Place: _____

    GRANDMOTHER'S MOTHER (Your maternal great-grandmother

    Maiden name: _____

    Born (date): _____Place: _____

    GRANDMOTHER'S FATHER (Your maternal great-grandfather)

    Name: _____

    Born (date): _____Place: _____

YOUR MOTHER'S FATHER (Your maternal grandfather)

Name: _____

Born (date): _____Place: _____

    GRANDFATHER'S FATHER (Your maternal great-grandfather)

    Name: _____

    Born (date): _____Place: _____

    GRANDFATHER'S MOTHER (Your maternal great-grandmother)

    Maiden name: _____

    Born (date): _____Place: _____

(Continue with Roots Questionnaire-2, Figure 8.)

FIGURE 7

ROOTS QUESTIONNAIRE–2

Information About Your Father's Side of the Family

YOUR FATHER

Name: _____

Born (date): _____Place: _____

Names of his brothers and sisters (your uncles and aunts):

_____

YOUR FATHER'S MOTHER (Your paternal grandmother)

Maiden name: _____

Born (date): _____Place: _____

GRANDMOTHER'S MOTHER (Your paternal great-grandmother

Maiden name: _____

Born (date): _____Place: _____

GRANDMOTHER'S FATHER (Your paternal great-grandfather)

Name: _____

Born (date): _____Place: _____

YOUR FATHER'S FATHER (Your paternal grandfather)

Name: _____

Born (date): _____Place: _____

GRANDFATHER'S FATHER (Your paternal great-grandfather)

Name: _____

Born (date): _____Place: _____

GRANDFATHER'S MOTHER (Your paternal great-grandmother)

Maiden name: _____

Born (date): _____Place: _____

On the other side of this sheet, write any interesting facts or stories about your parents, grandparents, and even great-grandparents. When did they come to this country? What is your nationality or country of origin? What kind of work did your ancestors do? How much education did they have? Are there any funny or sad stories about them that have been passed along in your family?

FIGURE 8

GENEALOGICAL CHART

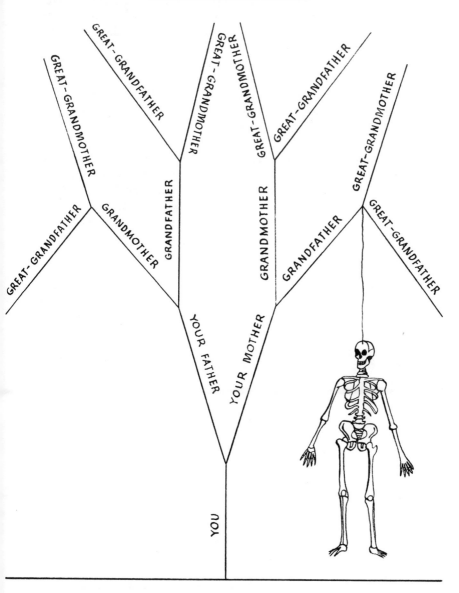

Note: In this unit we have freely mixed the "roots" and "branches" metaphors. If students prefer to think exclusively of roots, they merely have to turn this page upside down. Watch out for falling family skeletons.

FIGURE 9

Students will need to do considerable interviewing and perhaps launch a letter-writing campaign to people in more distant places to seek information. They may want to tape-record any live interviews with parents and other relatives. This is also the time to collect photos and to sift through other documents and records. (In teaching this unit ourselves, we found that parents often welcomed this kind of research and were delighted to have their children take on the task of sorting through, cataloging, and preserving family records that had gathered dust in the attic for years.)

While students are collecting or waiting for information, they can begin taking notes from history books (and possibly newspapers and magazines) that describe the time periods coinciding with their families' histories. For example, they might discover that their grandparents were married just before the Stock Market Crash, that an older brother or sister was born at the beginning of the Korean War. This, in turn, could lead to historical research on those eras.

Once students have collected their data, the last step of the prewriting stage is to plan how to organize and present the information. Have students sort through their materials to find the oldest names and dates, the next oldest information, and so on. Then they should begin correlating their relatives' recollections, experiences, and anecdotes with the factual information they have gathered. One way to do this is to write the dates and historical events on index cards and clip these to corresponding information from their relatives. Finally, students need to decide what information to include and exclude. They can discuss their ideas with a classmate to see which topics are most interesting to a potential reader. They may also write a one- or two-paragraph prospectus, broadly outlining their plan.

Writing

The writing of the *Family History Book* (or preparing a display or demonstration) consists principally of transcribing narratives and interviews from relatives and subsequently creating the commentary to help relate and explain the information. Students can do their transcribing at home, double-checking information or asking questions when necessary. They can do their commentaries in class, working with the teacher and other classmates to make certain that the historical dates are accurate and the relationships in the commentary are clear to their readers.

Revising

When students have completed their first drafts, they can present their projects to a small group and talk through their family history.

As they present their ideas, the group should ask questions and react to the presentation, perhaps using the response sheet shown in Figure 10 as a guide. This will help the writers discover what is clear and what is not, what needs to be developed or condensed. Alternatively the teacher can provide editorial advice along the same lines, with oral or written comments.

After groups have critiqued the papers, lead the class and individual writers in a guided discussion of how to go about revising their papers. Help them see possibilities by raising such questions as—

■ If you feel you need to work on the beginning, can you make it more interesting by telling a story? giving more historical background? using one of your own experiences while collecting material for the project? using quotes from an interview?

■ If your readers were confused or lost interest, can you delete some unnecessary material? add more commentary? rearrange the sequence of events? develop your stories more?

■ If the ending needs work, can you finish with an interesting anecdote? conclude with information from your family to tie the events together? close with a funny or powerful story or example? end with your own summary of the importance of your family history?

REVISION SHEET FOR FAMILY HISTORY PROJECT

1. While listening to or reading the presentation, jot down or point out the parts that most interested you or particularly attracted your attention.

2. After the presentation is finished, describe what impressed you most about the author's roots and the historical time periods covered. Summarize your impressions in a sentence or two.

3. Describe or point out to the author any section that seemed confusing to you or any time you lost interest in the presentation.

4. Jot down any questions you have about the material or write down the events, ideas, and personalities that you want to know more about.

5. Put yourself in the author's place and think what you might do to make this presentation ready for the next audience. What suggestions do you have to make the beginning, middle, and ending of the presentation more interesting or clear?

FIGURE 10

Copyediting

Give students strategies for checking grammar, spelling, and mechanics. For example, suggest that they—

■ Read the work aloud, either to themselves or to a friend. This will unearth a great many usage, editing, and punctuation problems.

■ Read the work backward, starting at the last word and working to the front. (This strategy forces the reader to look at every individual word without regard for content.)

■ Read through the paper several times, each time focusing on a different item such as spelling the first time, usage the second.

Copyediting can also take place in class, providing an opportunity for the teacher and class copyediting experts to give help as needed.

Presentation and Publication

After all the work, this project deserves to receive a great deal of public attention. The class can organize a Family History Night, either in school (possibly in conjunction with parents' night) or at a central location in the community such as the public library. Student writing with a community focus can also be submitted to local newspapers or community magazines for publication consideration. Whenever possible, copies of family histories should also be photocopied and mailed to relatives for their enjoyment. We have found that families often become so involved in the project that the development continues after the formal presentation, as various family members keep on presenting anecdotes and artifacts to one another.

Followup

Students can extend their historical research and writing skills beyond the project through some of the following:

■ Research cultural and social history by consulting local residents who can tell you about traditional practices in cooking, herbal and folk medicine, toymaking, furniture-making, musical instruments, and so on.

■ Write some historical pamphlets on your community. A local printer may be willing to subsidize the project, and the historical society will certainly be interested in having new topics explored.

■ Organize a historical walking tour for your community.

■ Sponsor an old-time fair that features canned/baked goods from old family recipes, dried herbs and foods, regional specialties, folk medicines, old-fashioned clothing, games and entertainment.

MATHEMATICS AND HUMANKIND

Brain researchers say that we do not "learn" anything new, but that the brain takes in new data and relates it to knowledge already stored in its memory banks. Writing in mathematics classes can reinforce this process as students combine theories and principles they are learning with their own experiences to create story problems, to determine how much something is worth, or to discover what it is like to develop an idea or theory that could change the world. The writing ideas suggested in this unit involve different calculations, careful observation, and making and testing hypotheses. Therefore, instead of working on isolated calculations, students will relate the information from class and their own experience to larger problems they will analyze and solve.

Content Objectives

■ To conceptualize mathematical principles and formulas by using them in written projects designed and developed by students.
■ To systematically relate the information given in class to students' existing knowledge.
■ To sharpen students' imaginative powers to analyze and solve problems.

Writing Ideas

Most of these projects require access to libraries, banking information, or the school's athletic directors and records. If teachers or students prefer shorter projects or options to written reports, we suggest poster displays, debates, and illustrated or oral presentations. For example, a math "minute-mystery" can be turned into a poster giving visual and written clues that lead an observer to a possible solution. Other subjects, such as reading, mathematics or intelligence testing can be the issue of a class debate or a *60 Minutes-*type exposé. Another possibility is preparing and presenting role-played interviews with mathematicians such as Einstein, Pythagorus, or Newton.

■ Read Arthur Conan Doyle's Sherlock Holmes story *The Musgrave Ritual* to see how this English detective used mathematics to help solve a murder mystery. Then try writing your own short story mystery using the information you are acquiring in class. Or try writing very short mystery problems that can be read within a minute—"minute-mysteries"—but that require mathematical solutions.

■ Look at the economy of another country and compare the prices of goods there with the prices of comparable items in this country. First determine the average exchange rate for the dollar; then examine the effects of inflation, average national income, and average hourly wage on the price of certain goods. How do you determine the *real* worth of a particular item? Try to devise a formula to do this.

■ Examine how mathematics is used in methods to evaluate and measure intelligence, reading skills, mathematical abilities, and other aptitudes. A book students should read is Bannesh Hoffman's *Tyranny of Testing* (Harper and Row, 1962) which explains our testing systems and their inaccuracies. Write an editorial for the school or local paper, or an exposé explaining what you have learned and expressing your opinions. Or devise alternatives to current testing programs.

■ For a historical view of mathematics, investigate the origins and conventions of measurement—of a triangle or the length of a day—and pretend you are the mathematician or scientist who developed the method. In a letter to a friend, how would you write about your discovery and excitement?

Or look at some of the new ways that have been developed for measuring things, such as the aerodynamics of cars or the energy of subatomic particles, and pretend you are the mathematician. In a press conference, how would you explain what you developed and why you did so? How do you think your idea/theory will affect the world?

■ Examine strategies and plays used by your football or basketball teams by taking into account the trajectories of passes and kicks, average running speeds of players, and the velocity of the ball. Then devise your own plays taking these variables into account—can you devise the perfect play or series of plays?

■ Think of everyday things that could or should be measured and devise a system for doing so. For example, how can you measure the productivity of a school day? the energy used in wasting time? How do you measure "hard work"? success? Or how do you measure different kinds of time—the time you experience when enjoying yourself versus the time you experience when bored? Does time have different speeds? Another option is measuring the aerodynamics of a person walking, running, swimming, skiing, skating, or biking. What should people wear or how should they move to go faster or more efficiently?

Writing and Learning

Prewriting

Students can complete projects for the first, third, and fourth options in class if teachers bring in many books and magazines relating to the subjects. To start any of the subjects or writing ideas, students should choose a subject, write what they already know about it, collect the appropriate information, and take notes from any sources they use. Once they finish gathering materials, have them fill out a project plan sheet to give them direction in preparing their first drafts (see Figure 11).

Writing and Revising

After students complete the project plan sheet and finish their first drafts, have them divide into small groups to present their ideas, drafts, and sketches. (Those who are working on minute-mysteries may prefer to work in pairs so that their mysteries remain semi-mysterious.) Students should read their drafts aloud, talk through their oral presentations, or describe and explain sketches. For each presentation, those listening to the project should fill out a brief critique that will serve as a guide to the writer in revising and rewriting (see Figure 12).

After the first revision session, the teacher can spend a class period or two with students spot-checking their work, offering suggestions, and answering questions. Also, some students may have to do additional research to further develop their ideas or to reinforce their purpose. Before starting their final rewriting and preparation of the projects, they should begin copyediting. Have three or four spelling-bee champions in one corner of the room and grammar experts in another acting as an editorial board that reads through and approves the projects. The teacher can also circulate through the room looking at papers and pointing out errors. Or students can work in small groups reading each other's work aloud or checking each project two or three times making sure to focus only on spelling the first time, grammar the second, and usage the third.

PROJECT PLAN SHEET

1. What is your subject? Explain why you are interested in it.

2. Describe your audience. Why should they know about your subject and how do you hope to affect them?

3. What information is critical to your audience's understanding of the subject and material you want to present? List. What information will your audience already know prior to the presentation?

4. Describe how you want to present your ideas. What form (editorial, poster, minute-mystery, etc.) is best for your ideas and what general outline should you follow to make your ideas clear?

5. Keeping in mind your answers to questions 1–4, try writing a first draft or sketching out your ideas for visual presentation. If you get stuck or need advice, have someone read your work and ask for suggestions.

FIGURE 11

REVISION GUIDE

1. As you listen to the presentation, jot down what you like best and are most interested in.

2. Write down any questions or general comments you have when the presentation ends.

3. Did you become confused or disinterested in any section? If so, identify the section and describe what happened to you.

4. Check any of the following revision methods that will help make the presentation more interesting or clearer to you:

   —Add more information or pictures (show where).

   —Take out confusing or unnecessary sections (point out).

   —Add an interesting fact, clue, story, or idea in the beginning that helps introduce the subject (make suggestions).

   —Change the order of the ideas or pictures (explain).

   —Add words, signals, or sentences that explain the order of ideas (show where).

   —Add words, signals, or sentences that help tie together your ideas and the information you present (point out where).

   —Give some of your own opinions, ideas, or conclusions (suggest where).

   —Add some interesting information or pictures at the end to reinforce your point (make suggestions).

FIGURE 12

Presentation and Publication

Students can share their work with the class, school, or community by—

■ Collecting and mimeographing written work for a class anthology.

■ Displaying posters and projects in the classroom, in the school library, or in local buildings or shopping centers.

■ Sending articles, stories, puzzles, or editorials to school or local newspapers.

■ Videotaping or recording live presentations for other mathematics classes.

Followup

Teachers and students who wish to do similar mathematics projects can choose any of the following:

■ Publish a fact book containing interesting mathematical information that people use consciously or subconsciously every day.

■ Compile and publish a statistical fact book for the school's athletic program. Besides wins, losses, averages, etc., include plays, energy expenditures, and so on.

■ Write letters to national testing programs, local colleges, school boards, or the PTA asking questions, giving opinions, and offering suggestions about the systems being used to evaluate and measure intelligence, reading, mathematical, and other aptitudes.

■ Write scripts for a radio or television series in which scientists and mathematicians from all historical ages discuss their views of the world and the future.

■ Develop math fairs that show how people use mathematics every day or how it affects our lives. Possible themes can include energy, money, the economy, or forensic medicine.

■ Form a financial planning group that gives advice to students on how to earn, save, and manage money. Or write a monthly money column for the school newspaper.

TRANSITIONS

Teenagers are naturally—almost obsessively—concerned with what is happening to their bodies as they grow up. Although acutely aware of the physical and emotional changes taking place, they cannot always understand and certainly cannot control them. With the added pressures imposed by peers to "look right" and "fit in," adolescence is often an extraordinarily difficult period.

Many times health and physical education units on human development do not reach students' deepest concerns. Doing "reports" on food groups, smoking, drugs, or human anatomy does not guarantee that students will learn much about themselves. In many cases, teachers may receive more or less similar reports cribbed from health pamphlets, while outside class, teenagers wonder what is happening to them.

This writing unit allows students to use their own experiences and knowledge to supplement basic research. The four stages in the unit can be shortened or lengthened to accommodate the teacher's goals and the students' needs. These stages carry the students from assessing their own experience through researching questions of special interest to writing and presenting their findings to a school or community audience.

Content Objectives

In this unit students will—

■ Study what is happening to their bodies and minds because of

1. the food they eat
2. the biological imperatives (what nature and genes make happen)
3. the psychological aspects of adolescence.

■ Integrate their own experiences with their understanding of human growth and development.
   ■ Supplement their experiences and knowledge with research.
   ■ Seek useful solutions to common teen problems.

Writing Ideas

Within each of the three general areas mentioned (food, biological imperatives, psychological needs) are a number of general topics for students to investigate. Under *food they eat*, for instance, they can look into such diverse matters as television advertising, preservatives and additives, pesticides in the food chain, drugs and hormones in meat, fast foods/junk foods, allergies, and fad diets. While exploring the *demands of growth* they can study growth rate and its effects on physical needs, the necessary calorie/carbohydrate/protein intake for teens, nutritional needs for those involved in sports, the dangers of sports to a growing teen, and what will happen to them physically in the next two, five, or twenty-five years. Looking at *psychological aspects*, they can consider how advertising shapes their self-image, pressures to fit in by consuming drugs and alcohol, psychological ailments common to teens (anorexia nervosa, depression, alcoholism), and prejudices against and pressures on people who do not have "ideal" bodies.

To develop any one of these topics, students can select from among the following options:

■ Write a brochure giving the background of a common teen problem as well as ways to solve or cope with the problem. Brochures can range from "The Care and Feeding of the Teenage Body" to "What to Do If You're Not the All-American Beach Teen."

■ Write a short story focusing on one of the subjects. Let it reflect your experiences, knowledge, and insights, but feel free to fictionalize—to make the story about somebody else and not completely true to life.

■ Prepare a restaurant or shopping guide for teenagers in your community who want to diet, improve their diet, avoid junk foods or food additives, or who have food allergies.

■ Create a poster display on one of the subjects. Those treating food topics can be hung in the school lunchroom; those on sports can be displayed in sports areas; and those looking into social issues can be placed in the school library or media center.

■ Write a radio script for a documentary program on one of the subjects. Tape-record your presentation and have it aired over the school public address system. Or arrange with a local radio station to use some or all of it for a public service program.

■ Write your own diet/exercise book.

■ Write a Dear Abby column for the class with letters and advice focusing on common teen dilemmas.

■ Write an editorial for the school paper on one of the topics.

Writing and Learning

Launch the unit by having students fill out (confidentially, of course) a questionnaire similar to the one shown in Figure 13. Although students need not reveal private or personal information, simply holding a class discussion after the questionnaire has been completed will bring a number of key topics out into the open. The teacher can list these potential topics and problems on the board, perhaps under the three headings suggested for the general organization of the unit: *food, biological imperatives, psychological needs and pressures*.

From this questionnaire students should have enough information for a ten- or fifteen-minute free writing exercise to help them focus on a particular topic they wish to explore further. At this point, present a list of specific writing options (radio scripts, poster displays, etc.) and have students zero in on both a topic and a mode of presentation.

Prewriting

Each student can now plan an individual program of research. Typically, when faced with a research question, students promptly head for the encyclopedia for a summary of the basic facts. Although it is not likely that teachers can control the use of books, we would suggest that they strongly encourage students to look for other sources and to draw on the encyclopedia only as a last resort. Among the information sources students can explore are the following:

- The class textbook
- Books, magazines, and pamphlets from the local or school library
- Monographs and leaflets from doctors' offices
- Write-away materials from food processors, fast food chains, etc.
- Area people involved in medicine, psychology, sports or physical fitness, farming, and food processing
- Audiovisual materials from local libraries or companies.

A few days after beginning the unit, ask each student to turn in a one- or two-page prospectus on the topic, including a description of the major questions to investigate and a list of special resources to examine. This is a good time for the teacher to provide input in the form of specific advice and suggestions, places to look for information, even book or magazine titles. Time spent evaluating the prospectus helps ensure success and considerably reduces the amount of time spent in evaluating the final paper.

QUESTIONS ON ADOLESCENCE

Questions about FOOD:

1. What foods do you eat most often? Why?

2. Does advertising influence what you eat or where you eat?

3. Where do you go out to eat most often? Why?

4. Are you conscious of the vitamins/minerals or additives in what you eat?

5. Have you noticed any changes in your eating habits in the last year?

6. Have you ever gone on a special diet or eating program? Why? Did a doctor give you advice on it?

7. How would you describe your general physical health? Do you suffer from any particular problems such as insomnia, stomach aches, food allergies, fatigue, nervousness?

Questions about BIOLOGICAL IMPERATIVES

1. When did you physically start to come of age? When did you first notice bodily changes? What was your response?

2. Do you feel you developed more slowly or more rapidly than most other people your age?

3. Do you participate in exercise programs to try to get or keep your new body in shape?

4. Do you feel you have a good body, a poor body, or an average body?

5. Do you know what changes will take place in your body next?

6. If you could go through the changes of adolescence all over again, what requests would you make of Mother Nature?

7. Do you have unanswered questions about what is happening to your body or what will happen to it in the near future?

Questions about SOCIAL AND PSYCHOLOGICAL PRESSURES

1. What do you think the average teenager should look and act like? Why?

2. Does advertising reinforce or affect these views? How?

3. How do you fit your own definition?

4. What are the most common social conflicts or worries that you face daily?

5. What pressures from society do you feel and respond to?

6. If you were to write a Dear Abby letter, what problem would you want advice about?

FIGURE 13

Writing and Revising

As stressed at the beginning of this unit, for it to succeed, students must not simply regurgitate their book learning as they compose reports. As they move toward writing their papers, remind them that their *personal* reaction, response, and interpretation are important. First person pronouns are perfectly acceptable (students may have been inappropriately taught to avoid "I" in an English class), and their writing should be chatty and anecdotal if they want it to be.

The following questions encourage such personal writing:

- What is your unique point of view on the subject?
- What are your personal experiences with the subject? Is there any reason not to use them in your paper?
- Who is the audience of the paper? If that audience were here, right now, what specifically would you like to tell it?
- In what ways did your reading or other research help you understand your own experience better?
- Did your reading correct any mistaken beliefs you had?
- Did the reading fail to answer some specific questions? Why?

Then students should draft, preferably in class. While they are working, the teacher can quickly check their plans, make suggestions, and provide help. If students get stuck, encourage them to talk out their ideas and problems with teacher or peers or to skip over the troublesome spots and go on with the rest of the project.

When students have finished their drafts, lead a class discussion based on what they have learned or let them present or read their work to small groups. Distribute a revision sheet similar to the one shown in Figure 14 to guide group members in evaluating the projects and making recommendations to the author.

Presentation and Publication

The revision sheets provide resources for a revised copy of the project. (The teacher may want to offer advice at this point, too.) Then students should rewrite and copyedit, preparing clean copy for whichever form of presentation they have chosen. As suggested under Writing Ideas, this unit leads to a variety of publication and presentation modes, from radio broadcasts to poster displays. Most important is that the student receive some audience recognition for his/her work. Further, for the benefit of other adolescents in *transition*, the public presentation of this material seems especially important. At the end of this unit, other students can learn genuinely important lessons from these writer/learners.

REVISION SHEET FOR TRANSITIONS PROJECT

1. Underline or point out what you liked best about the draft of the paper or project.

2. Are you convinced or persuaded that the author's viewpoints are valid and accurate? Explain what you learned from the project. List points where you disagreed and explain why.

3. Check any of the following that could strengthen the presentation:

    —Give more background information.
    —Provide more facts, percentages, statistics, etc.
    —Develop examples more.
    —Use more personal examples.
    —Other: _____

4. Indicate whether any of the following need to be changed:

    —Rearrange the order (explain how).
    —Delete confusing sentences (point out).
    —Add sentences that emphasize the order of ideas (show where).
    —Add sentences or words that explain what the author is trying to accomplish (show where).

FIGURE 14

Followup

Some additional writing ideas based on the unit topics include the following:

■ Look at alternative eating styles: American Indian, Chinese, Afro-American, South American, French, Italian, Chicano, etc., and write a comparative paper. Or create an international cookbook based on the ethnic backgrounds of students in the school containing recipes your classmates contribute. (This can be a good fundraiser as well.)

■ Create an *Almanac and Book of Facts* about the makeup and amazing capabilities of the human body.

■ Do product evaluations for food. Test individual brands for quality. Do they live up to their advertising claims? Figure out which foods on the market are the best buys and why. Write a report for other students to read or write your opinions directly to the companies.

■ Rewrite magazine advertisements to sell products, not an idealized image of what an American teen should look, act, or think like. Write letters to companies critiquing their advertising.

COMPUTER LITERACY

Computers show every sign of being far more than a fad or a craze. It seems accurate to say that the present generation is the "computer generation," and that these youngsters will grow up employing computers casually in ways undreamt of by their elders. However, the computer children will need to be more than button pushers, more than passive consumers of computer hardware and software. This unit explores the ways in which language study and computers "interface," helping students enhance their understanding of computers and their "computer literacy." The first part of the unit involves students in studying about computers. The second part has them use a computer to write an essay (or, if a computer is not available, has them simulate one to learn editing skills).

Note: The unit does not require the teacher to be computer literate. It can be a useful self-teaching exercise for the teacher who does not know much about computers and wants to learn more.

Part I. Computers and Language

There are several different levels of computer literacy. At the very lowest or most basic level, one merely needs to know how to put a quarter into a Pac-Man arcade game or how to insert the identification card into a Magic Teller in order to interact with a computer. More sophisticated computerphiles not only use machines by pressing buttons, but have some understanding of how they work.

Part I takes students (and indirectly, the teacher) at their present level of literacy and lets them expand it by learning from books and writing about computers.

Writing Ideas

■ Learn something about the history of computers, how they began as "analytical engines" in the previous century, how they evolved as huge machines in the 1940s and 1950s, how they gradually were miniaturized into the form of TRS-80s and PETs and Apples—the computers found at school and at home. Prepare a monograph on the evolution of the computer.

■ Learn something about a computer "language," probably the one called BASIC which is used on most home computers. What does it mean to "talk" to a computer? What are the special words used in a language like BASIC? What happens if you misspell a word in BASIC? What happens if you omit a punctuation mark? If you can bring a computer into the classroom, give a demonstration of how BASIC works. Otherwise, prepare some posters showing how the language works.

■ Many computers seem to "talk" to you by asking questions and replying to your answers:

Computer: What is your name?
You: Sharon Q. Public.
Computer: Hello, Sharon Q. Public, nice to meet you.

How do they do that? Read and report to the class.

■ Read about applications of small computers in various parts of everyday life and make a report to the class, written or oral, about "Computers in Our Future." Some of the areas to investigate are the following:

Home Finance   Home Management
Sports   Hobbies
Schoolwork   Games

■ Study the home computers on the market and write a "Consumer Reports" booklet on the various makes. Which ones are the best buys? Which ones are the most useful? Which ones have the biggest supply of software? Which one would you buy?

■ If you have some experience writing programs (or if you just want to learn how) study a book on BASIC programming and write a program for something like games or math problems. Show the class how your program works. Describe the "bugs" you found in your program and how you learned to "debug" the computer by talking its language.

■ Write a short story about the use and misuse of computers—for example, a story about how computers can be programmed to "steal" from other computers. Be sure, however, that your facts are accurate.

Or

Write a science fiction story about superintelligent computers, making certain it is within the realm of possibility, not just wildly fantastic.

■ Study some other computer "languages" such as art and music. How does a computer draw intricate graphic patterns? How does it "learn" to play and compose music? How do you program a computer to do these things? Explain to the class how a programmer can go from an idea in his/her head to creating music and art through a computer.

■ Study talking computers. How is a voice generated electronically in a computer? Learn about digitalizing devices that can turn human speech into language the computer can understand. Write a report about the possible applications of talking computers. (Or, using two tape recorders, put on a simulation of how computers can talk to each other.)

Writing and Learning

Prewriting

Prepare for this unit by stocking a supply of books on computers; in all probability the school and public libraries have many titles. Students who are interested in computers can most likely supply back issues of some of the popular computer magazines such as *Creative Computing* and *Interface Age*. Add to this library by procuring catalogs and other promotional literature about computers from a computer supply store. (While there, teachers can introduce themselves to the sales representative and describe the unit they are teaching. Computer salespeople are eager to demonstrate products in schools; thus it may be possible to lead off the unit with a professional presentation about the dimensions of personal computing.)

When the class library is ready, introduce the writing topics, ask for other suggestions, and get students started reading. Whether or not teachers are computer literate, they can bring expertise to the unit by helping students find the materials they need. Again, because so many students have experience with computers, teachers may well find the class taken over by those with expertise. So much the better.

This unit does not absolutely require a computer in the classroom. However, the quality of the unit would be better if at least one unit were available for students to work with—for example, a common machine such as a Radio Shack TRS-80, an Apple, or a Commodore PET or VIC-20, together with a few math and English programs and games. Then students who are planning to write programs for their project can do so in class.

Part II. Word Processing

Writing and Revising

If a computer is available for use in the unit, try to get one with an elementary word processing program. (The phrase "word processing" sounds very dehumanized. In fact, word processors are anything but automatic, and they do *not* take the creativity or the hard work out of writing.)

Plan A (with a word processor). Have students do their drafts and revisions on the computer, learning how to use the program to make changes in their manuscripts. Preliminary research shows that access to a word processor encourages students to revise, since they need not rewrite "clean copy" every time they make a change in the manuscript. Further, there is tremendous satisfaction in seeing finished text flow out of a printer at high speed.

If the class has only one computer, schedule its use carefully so that every student can work with it. In such cases, drafting may have to be done with paper and pencil as usual, with only the final copy done on the computer. When students have access to three or four machines, it is relatively easy for everyone to use the hardware. (Again, check with a computer supply store about free demonstrations. It may be possible to arrange for the free use of machines for a week or more.)

Plan B (without a word processor). Whether or not students can work with a machine, it is important to note that for the immediate future, most people will *not* have word processors to use on a daily basis. The original word processor—the pencil—will remain in vogue for at least a few decades more. Further, students can learn something about paper and pencil editing from word processing programs. For example, students often confuse *revising* with *copyediting*; they think that revising means recopying their papers correcting spelling errors. Word processing programs provide a graphic demonstration of the four basic processes of revising: *adding* (words, phrases, paragraphs); *deleting* (words, phrases, paragraphs); *substituting* (one word or phrase for another); and *rearranging* (moving sections around). These four steps can be done almost as easily with paper and pencil as they can on a computer. In fact, many changes can be made much more rapidly and efficiently on "hard copy" than on the computer screen.

Teach students these four functions. One way to do this is to type several paragraphs—of teacher or student writing—on an overhead transparency and lead the group through an editing session, taking each of the four word processing operations in turn. What do we

57

want to *add* to this writing? What should we *delete*? Are there *substitutions*—better choices of language? Can we *rearrange* to make things clearer?

Finally, let students "word process" their own compositions, after first exchanging papers and collecting the advice of peers. At this time, too, point out that computers are basically "dumb" machines. They cannot edit a writer's work for him/her. They cannot determine what is a "good" deletion or addition or whether rearranging a paragraph makes any sense. No computer will ever write an "A" paper, although it may make it simpler for the author to complete the writing process successfully.

Followup

■ Have students do a survey of available computer software in your discipline. New programs are coming out daily that are useful to history, social studies, English, science, mathematics, and vocational education teachers. Many of these programs are of very low quality; some are excellent. Give students the task of finding out which work best.

■ Describe the programs you would like to see developed for your class or subject matter and let the students who are skilled programmers develop them.

■ Have several students investigate the new "spell guard" programs that search out typographical errors and correct them. How do these new language programs work?

■ Encourage a group to research some of the new editing programs being developed by the Bell Laboratories and report to the class.

■ Encourage students who are familiar with computers to prepare a primer for the class on other computer languages: FORTRAN, Pascal, LISP, etc. Have them explain to the class how these differ from BASIC.

■ Can a computer be programmed to translate a foreign language? Set a study group to the task.

■ Can a computer be used to keep a writer's diary or journal? Have a study group look for programs that do this.

■ How are computers used on newspapers? Arrange for a group of students to visit a computerized newspaper to learn the relationship between computer composing and typesetting.

Part III

Applications and Extensions

SUMMARY OF PRINCIPLES

1. Keep content at the center of the writing process, addressing yourself to *what* the writing says, allowing *how it says it* to be treated incidentally.

2. Make certain students know their material before writing: content understanding shines through in student writing.

3. Design writing activities that help students structure and synthesize their knowledge, not merely regurgitate it.

4. Provide audiences for student writing, real or imaginary, so that students have a sense of writing for someone other than the teacher.

5. Look for writing activities that allow the student to play the roles of *learner* and *researcher.*

6. Teach the *process* of writing:
   a. Spend much time with prewriting, helping students acquire a solid grasp of the material.
   b. Provide assistance and support as students write, helping them solve problems as they arise, rather than waiting until they turn in the paper.

7. Let students revise one another's papers. Provide support through revision checklists and guidelines.

8. Don't confuse revising with copyediting:
   a. Teach revision first, having students clarify the content and substance of their work.
   b. Turn to copyediting of spelling, mechanics, usage, etc., only in the final phases of writing.

9. Display or otherwise publicize student writing through shows, demonstrations, book publishing (duplicated or one-of-a-kind), oral readings. Don't be the only reader of your students' work.

10. **Keep content at the center of the writing process.**

FINDING TOPICS

"What can I write about?" is students' perennial lament. The teacher's variation of that theme is, "What shall I have them write about?" That teacher concern helps explain the popularity of books that provide laundry lists of topics and ideas for youngsters' writing, inviting the teacher to pick a topic virtually at random for the next writing assignment. We prefer a more systematic approach to writing and content teaching and think that if students are to grow as both writers and learners, there has to be some rhyme and reason to the sequence of topics they study.

We have discovered that if teachers take the sort of interdisciplinary approach described in Parts I and II of this book, topics for writing and learning appear everywhere. Each day something happens at school or in the world at large that lends itself to content writing—"Wouldn't it be interesting to have students write about *that*?"

For the newcomer to writing in the content areas, the textbook—whether science, social studies, mathematics, or other subject—provides the logical place to start the search for topics. Each new chapter in the book provides a source of potential writing ideas.

In discussing textbooks, however, we need to mention one of our biases quickly: most of the reading, writing, and discussion topics supplied by commercial textbooks are poorly designed. Textbook writers violate most of the principles of content-area teaching we have described. Too often the topics stress memorization and regurgitation; they seldom build in any provision for an audience; too often they lead to "homework writing" that is boring to write and read.

Some of those topics can be salvaged, however, by simply applying good content-writing principles. For example, a science book presents the following as a "study assignment":

> Write a report on the ingredients contained in a number
> of common household products and how they work.

Such an assignment invites bad writing because it seems aimless, without focus, and lacking in audience. We would rewrite it something like this:

> Make a search of the cleaning cabinet around your home
> or apartment—the place where all the cleaning supplies
> are kept. Choose two or three products that are used

around your home regularly—detergent, rug shampoo, floor wax—and copy the ingredients from the label. Then, based on your study in this unit, write a paragraph or two about each product, explaining to your parents (or whoever uses the products) just why they work as they do.

Another assignment in the same book reads simply:

Write a report on the life of Niels Bohr.

Instead, the teacher can say:

I've brought in a number of biographies of famous scientists (including Niels Bohr). I'd like you to read one of them and then do some writing about the person's life. Don't just summarize what the person did; instead choose an important moment in that person's life and write a dramatic scene (or short story) about it. We'll act them out (or read them aloud) to the class.

Thus a number of textbook concepts can be covered through interdisciplinary writing. Further, teachers will find that if they adapt textbook topics in this way, their students will learn the material more successfully than they have in the past.

Curriculum guides, although little more than listings of fundamental concepts to be covered at each grade level, can often supply ideas for content-area writing. To convert one of these concepts to writing ideas, look for "the literacy connection" and ask yourself, "How can that concept best be expressed through writing?" Then return to Part I of this publication, "A Primer on Teaching Writing in the Content Areas," and develop the concept as a writing topic.

The daily newspaper is filled with potential ideas for content-area writing. While browsing through the paper, teachers can often find news stories that are immediately relevant to their planned content teaching for the day. The news stories, in turn, can lead to writing that ranges in complexity from a simple journal response to daily events to a full-scale inquiry-centered unit on a key issue or topic of the day.

Similarly, newsmagazines can provide a wealth of ideas for content-area writing. The science or education or medicine or world events sections of such periodicals will probably not only contain ideas for writing, but some prewriting resources as well.

Other popular magazines can provide a starting point for writing in the content areas. English teachers discovered years ago that by talking to the local paperback/magazine distributor, they could often arrange to have out-of-date magazines supplied to their classes at no cost. Other teachers can probably arrange to receive magazines from *Ranger Rick's Nature Magazine* to *Popular Photography* in their classrooms at more or less regular intervals. These specialized magazines, in turn, can trigger the development of interdisciplinary writing lessons and units.

Learn to look for the real-world connection between what you are teaching (and what students might write about) and events in the school neighborhood, the community, and the state. Issues and concerns of day-to-day living have a tendency *not* to be easily classifiable by discipline. Therefore study of an issue such as ecology, or town planning, or the water supply will naturally cut across many disciplines in the humanities, sciences, and vocational fields. And writing, in turn, underlies all of these areas.

James Beck, a teacher at the University of Wisconsin, Whitewater, has his college students systematically look at how different disciplines view common issues and problems, forcing them to take an interdisciplinary perspective.[2] We tried this same idea with a group of Michigan teachers, exploring the topic of The Elderly from as many different points of view and from as many different interdisciplinary perspectives as possible. We reprint their list *in toto* just to show how exhaustive such a list can be and how easy it is to develop one.

THE ELDERLY

Science

■ How old do various animals live to be? Which animal has the longest lifespan? Which one has the briefest lifespan? Prepare a chart or display showing these relative lifespans.

■ What happens to cells when they grow old? Why don't we continue to grow new cells forever? Read about the aging of cells or conduct experiments and present your findings.

■ Do you share any of your grandparents' personality or physical traits? Interview your parents and study family photographs to discover resemblances. How do these come about? Prepare a photo-display to prove your points.

■ Read about or interview a doctor on lifelong eating habits. What does your eating style determine about the length of your life?

■ Explore cryogenics and the possibility of freezing sick people and reviving them later when cures for their diseases are known. Present your findings in a report or possibly a realistic science fiction story.

Mathematics

■ How many people are alive on planet earth now? How old are they? Design a world map showing population centers and the approximate percentages of people in various age brackets.

■ Trace the increasing average life expectancy in the United States from colonial times to the present. Prepare a display or a talk showing what has happened. What does science/mathematics project to be the average lifespan 50 or 100 years from now?

■ Formulate a year's budget for a person over 65 taking into account social security benefits. How difficult is it for an elderly person to get along financially in retirement?

■ Explore the statistics on food production in the world today. Where does the world's food come from? Who consumes the most food? Who eats the least amount? Prepare the copy for a television or radio program that explores some of the problems of world hunger.

Art and Music

■ Study the photographs of the elderly in *The Family of Man*. What did the camera "see" in these people? Translate your impressions into words.

■ Read the biographies and autobiographies of artists who were still creating late in life: Picasso, Casals, Toscanini, O'Keeffe, Nevelson. What kept them going? Prepare a class presentation on some of these artists.

■ Study the ways in which the elderly are portrayed in paintings. What clues does a painter provide to show that a person is old? Then make some photographs of older people. Are the artists correct?

Social Science

■ Prepare a report on the various social care programs for the elderly: social security, medicare, medicaid, retirement plans. Write a position paper or editorial on the subject.

■ Investigate how different countries and cultures take care of the elderly. Then prepare an evaluation of such care in the United States.

■ Write an imaginary scene between a person who is about to enter a home for the elderly and his or her son or daughter. How does the elderly person feel? How does the "child" feel?

■ Find out if there is an adopt-a-grandparent program in your community and begin corresponding with a person in a home for the elderly.

History/Social Studies

■ Research the American Indian treatment of their elderly and write a monograph or report for the class.

■ Visit a home for the elderly and conduct a series of interviews with residents about what life was like during their youth. Use this information to compile a study of a period in twentieth century U.S. history.

■ Put yourself in the role of a person who lived in an earlier era and have him or her visit our society today. What would, say, Eleanor or Franklin Roosevelt think about the modern-day United States? What would George Washington think? Present this as a dramatic monologue for the class.

■ Locate an elderly person who is practicing a dying art or craft. Ask the person to teach you the basics of the craft, and use the ideas in an article, perhaps with photographs.

Civics

■ Research the history of the Gray Panthers, a group of advocates for the elderly, and describe their plans and programs.

■ Invite your local state representative to speak to the class describing current legislative proposals concerning the elderly. Write questions for the legislator to answer, and after the program, write letters to him or her describing your position on the proposed laws.

■ Research the laws and regulations concerning the establishment of homes for the elderly. What kinds of permits and credentials are required? Analyze these requirements. How do these rules and regulations protect the elderly?

■ Try to find out why U.S. senators are frequently elderly men, older than obligatory retirement age for most people. Are these men wiser than the rest of the population? (Similarly, study the age of various U.S. presidents. Can an elderly person be a successful ruler of a country?)

■ Do you think the elderly should have a right to die when they wish? Study the question and write a pro and con discussion, airing both sides of the issue. Then describe your own position. (Or study the subject of *euthanasia*, mercy killing, and write a similar paper.)

Vocational/Career Education

■ Learn about careers for the elderly and write a guidebook that would be helpful to an older person, about to retire, in finding something interesting and worthwhile to do.

■ Look into careers that involve the elderly: being a gerontologist (doctor for the elderly), running a community recreation center, and so forth. Prepare a display showing these career choices and giving their qualifications.

■ Interview an elderly person, perhaps one of your grandparents, on his/her feelings about working and a career. How do people feel about various kinds of work after spending a lifetime in such activity?

■ What is "lifelong education"? Where does one get it? What is important about it? Can you see yourself being involved in lifelong education after you have finished school or college?

Other Subjects and Disciplines

■ *Athletics.* Write a booklet describing various sports and other athletic activities that the elderly can enjoy.

■ *Technology.* Study *bionics*, the science of "mechanical" replacement parts for the body, and write a description of how this may affect aging during your lifetime.

■ *Futurism.* Consider the effects of research into DNA and the possible production of antibodies to protect the aged from diseases.

■ *Religion.* What do some elderly people you have interviewed believe about life after death? How have their attitudes changed as they have grown older?

The list can go on and on. Depending on the makeup of the class, a selected half-dozen or more of these topics can create a solid unit lasting several weeks. A broader selection can yield interesting activities stretching over a month or more.

But for those who would like additional suggestions for topics, one more list follows.

MORE IDEAS
FOR CONTENT-WRITING PROJECTS
IN SENIOR HIGH SCHOOL

Going to College

Getting a Job

Getting Married

Getting Divorced

Old Age and Youth

Cryogenics and Immortality

Rescues

Bacteria

Mountain Sports

Electrons

Lawyers

What's Basic?

Archaeology

What's a Classic?

Silicon Chips

The Bible

Politics

Science and Religion

Human Rights

The Military

All-Americans

Eyeglasses and Contacts

Meditation and Hypnotism

The Holocaust

Multicultural Values

Evaluating Things and People

The Human Heart

Right Brain/Left Brain

Virtue and Vice

War and Peace

Love and Money

Trivia

The Fifties (or any decade)

Herstory

Utopia

The Ideal School

Clones

Consumerism

World Religions

World Languages

World Values

The Justice System

Crime

Alcohol and Drugs

Privacy

Mental Health

EVALUATION AND GRADING
OF CONTENT WRITING

We have stressed the value of peer revision as an essential part of the writing process (see Part I). Although this helps dramatically reduce the theme-correcting burden, the fact remains that most teachers feel a need to make some comments, either written or oral, about student papers. As noted elsewhere, we suggest focusing the comments on *content*, stressing "writing" only as it affects the clear presentation of that content. These comments, then, should include such considerations as whether or not the paper successfully communicates the basic ideas, adequately defines terms, and is easily understandable to the proposed audience. Most research in writing suggests that at this stage, praise is far more helpful than criticism, and the most useful comments are those that not only point out things well done, but explain to the student *why* they were well done.

Grading is one form of evaluation that teachers must also deal with. It may be tempting for the teacher interested in writing in the content areas to give a double grade: one for content and one for writing quality. We recommend against this practice—although acknowledging its popularity among teachers—because it creates an unnecessary schism between writing and content. Instead, we suggest that the teacher apply content criteria—Are the facts right? Are the observations sound? Is the message accurate?—and focus on writing only as it enhances or detracts from the content. Thus the teacher can lavish high praise (and a good grade) on a paper that not only presents sound information, but does so articulately and even artistically. Likewise, if a paper is sloppily revised and carelessly spelled, the author should know that poor writing interfered with comprehension and resulted in a lower grade.

Grading should be relatively easy and painless if an assignment has been carefully designed and explained to students. In the course of prewriting, students will discuss what it is they are expected to include in their papers and the audience for their writing. The time spent on prewriting, then, is actually the beginning of the evaluation process. Further, if the teacher monitors their progress throughout the drafting, revising, and copyediting stages, students will have received considerable advice informally. The final grades in such assignments should therefore come as no great surprise to anyone.

An even better approach is to place writing on a pass/fail or credit/no credit basis. This eliminates pressure about grades and allows both student and teacher to concentrate on the quality of the writing and the content material. In a P/F or Cr/NCr system, minimum standards must be clearly articulated, and students must know that the teacher will not automatically accept any piece of writing they submit. In our experience with these systems, we have always used "best effort" as a measure: if students feel they have given their best work, and if we, as teachers, intuitively feel they have, then we accept a paper.

In a related kind of grading, the contract system, papers are similarly given credit/no credit, with the total number of papers submitted as a guide to the final grade. Despite an inherent weakness of emphasizing quantity over quality, the contract system works well if standards and criteria of evaluation are stated clearly.

It is crucial for teachers of writing in the content areas to recall that *grading* is not the same as *evaluation*. Although we believe the impact of grades on student writing should be minimized (or eliminated if possible), this is not to say that student writing should not be evaluated. Much of the evaluation should come through the peer group revising and copyediting sessions—where young writers get a real sense of how their writing affects real readers. But the teacher obviously must enter into the evaluation process, too. Sometimes this can be done through written comments on papers, which is time-consuming. Another method is the miniconference conducted on the spot—a minute or two spent in class discussing a part or all of a paper. Evaluation also comes when students submit their writing to public scrutiny by publication or display or oral reading to a group of peers or adults. It is unfortunate that grades too often substitute for these more substantial forms of evaluation.

Traditionally, writing evaluation has given most emphasis to mistakes and errors in content, mechanics, and usage. It is important to emphasize that students learn both writing and subject matter best when they *succeed* at what they have set out to do and when someone helps them understand why they have succeeded. Thus, in responding to and evaluating student writing, be lavish with praise for things well done rather than despairing of students' writing failures. Itemizing every fault on a student paper seldom produces positive growth and can be destructive of morale and self-confidence. This is not to imply that one should spare the rod and spoil the child. If a paper fails to communicate successfully, a student ought to know it. But, to use another cliche', nothing succeeds like success.

In the end, the best evidence of the success of a student's writing (or the success of a writing program) is in the writing itself. We strongly recommend that teachers initiate a *portfolio system* for maintaining copies of student writing (including notes and drafts, if they are of interest to the teacher). Such portfolios, carefully maintained for a semester or a year, provide evidence of student growth, in content mastery as well as in writing. Further, portfolios can provide useful material for discussion with parents and for conferences with individual students. A portfolio is better than an individual paper for diagnosing a student's writing problems and seeking solutions. And it can be handed along to teachers at the next grade level to provide some continuity of both content and writing instruction from one year to the next.

Some schools and districts may be interested in creating evaluation programs for all their students; in this age of accountability, a number of such systems have been developed. Usually they involve collecting writing samples on a pre- and post-test basis, after which teachers work in teams either to assess the writing *holistically* (making impressionistic judgments about such qualities as form, structure, style, and correctness), or to evaluate *primary traits* (searching for particular characteristics of good writing). Faculties engaging in such programs often report a greatly increased awareness of the importance of writing and of the strengths and weaknesses of their students' writing. For a detailed description of these approaches to schoolwide evaluation, as well as practical teaching pointers on the whole question of theme grading and evaluation, see Maxwell and Judy.[11]

EXAMINATIONS IN THE CONTENT AREAS: WRITING THEM/PREPARING STUDENTS FOR THEM

Most of the projects suggested thus far can be considered medium to long-range. They require a minimum of two to three days to complete, and often will extend over a period of several weeks or even a month. We want to reemphasize the principle that teaching content through writing does require *time*; one cannot simply ask students to dash off a piece of writing and expect that they will produce quality material.

However, there are occasions in school and in life when students are asked to produce writing on short notice, frequently under constraints of time and length. In both school and life these occasions fall under the rubric of "examinations," formal and informal, and they have certain common traits:

- The assignment is often highly specific.
- The writer needs to prove him/herself to an audience, demonstrating mastery of the topic.
- Although the writer may have had time to prepare the subject-matter knowledge required, there is little time for careful pre-writing planning (and there may be little time for revision as well).

Examples of such occasions are as follows:

Students: Please discuss current theories of the origin of life and describe the evidence to support each.

69

All Teachers: Send a description of your efforts to improve writing in your classes to Principal Conklin by noon Friday, making certain that you show how you have met the district-wide list of minimum skills.

Jenkins: Write a report for me on the Harrison trust and be quick about it.

It is important for middle/junior high and senior high school teachers to help their students prepare to write under such "fire-drill" conditions," for writing examinations is crucial to academic success and to success beyond schooling. At the same time, many examinations and examination situations are detrimental to good writing instruction; if not handled carefully, they can actually destroy the positive effects of a writing in the content areas program. Too many merely call for regurgitation of factual information or ask students to answer impossibly complex questions in short periods. Under pressure, students wilt: their natural writing voice disappears; they turn to murky phrases to cover their feelings of unpreparedness. In short, they produce the sort of writing that makes teachers turn to multiple-choice tests as a comprehensible alternative to essay writing.

It is possible, however, to design essay examinations in the content areas that make it easier for students to produce good writing. This is not to suggest that the examination itself should be made simpler (although in some instances, examinations that are meant to "challenge" students merely baffle them). But it makes sense for the teacher—content area or language arts—to try to create a situation where students produce their *best* writing, not their worst, and where they display their content knowledge as fully and clearly as they are able. The advice and precepts that follow contain the fundamental principles of content-area writing discussed in previous sections. In preparing written examinations, then, the teacher merely needs to recall the principles of good writing instruction and apply them as much as possible to the somewhat limited writing situation of the examination.

For instance, in designing a content examination, *consider the possibility that students can write in different discourse modes.* There is no reason to require students to display their knowledge only in expository prose such as an essay. Why not have general science students write a *dialogue* between an astronomer and a lay person to display their knowledge? Or have mathematics students write their own *story problem* and then solve it to demonstrate mastery of a concept? Or have history students compose an *on-the-*

scene report of the Battle of Britain or the Siege of Troy? Or have literature students compose an *interview with an author* instead of writing the usual literary analysis of the author's works?

Adding such a creative twist to examinations is more than a matter of novelty. In most cases, offering a specific discourse mode or writing possibility helps the teacher build *audience* and *purpose.* Instead of writing for the teacher just to display knowledge gleaned from a course, the student focuses that knowledge in a specific language form and writes for an audience, even though the audience may well be imaginary. Such examination topics invariably increase the amount of student involvement in writing, with observable improvement in clarity, organization, and voice. (Try a simple experiment: Give one class the usual essay assignment and another class a topic with a different discourse mode, with audience and purpose built in. Compare the writing quality.)

Further, to increase the probability that students will "make contact" with an essay question, include several options. Almost any content knowledge can be expressed clearly and fully in different ways. Although a student *might* write an on-the-scene report about Troy, he or she could also write about it in the form of a *letter* (either as a Greek or a Trojan, or as an exchange of letters between leaders of the two forces). The examination question might also be answered in the form of a *scenario* for a television or film documentary or even as a *fictionalized story* about life within the walls of Troy.

In other words, *examinations should encourage synthesis rather than recitation*; the value of an essay examination should be to allow students to discover their knowledge about a topic, not just to display it. It is equally important for the teacher to state clearly and articulately the expectations for the writing and what students need to do to complete it successfully. We prefer to put examinations on a pass/fail basis, telling our students how we will determine a passing examination. When grading is used—either out of personal preference or school-dictated necessity—it is also important to articulate clearly and precisely how the grade will be determined. Whether pass/fail or graded, any examination we write includes the criterion of *clear writing*; we make it plain to students that the examination is a "test" of their writing, not just of their knowledge. Nor do we find that the emphasis on writing quality distracts students from content; since the content and its expression are inseparable, the focus on writing also helps students clarify their content knowledge.

Finally, we think it important for the teacher to *build the steps of the writing process* into the examination. Of course, in a fifty-minute or even an hour-and-a-half examination, the process must be

71

severely condensed, but the teacher should nevertheless make provision for *prewriting, writing,* and *revision.* This can be done as part of the written instructions or through a brief oral presentation at the beginning of the examination.

However, there may be many times in school when students take examinations under less-than-ideal conditions, when the teacher does not build in audience or purpose or options. In such instances, the task is clear: students should write about what they know and write clearly.

To this end, we suggest that our students apply what they know about the writing process to the examination, however brief it may be, not allowing a great deal of time for planning. We tell them to split the available time into three portions: a brief time for prewriting, a longer time for writing, and a short time for revision and copyediting. Then we give them the following list of strategies:

Prewriting

1. Make certain to read the examination question carefully. Know exactly what is being asked of you. Underline the key words and phrases in the assignment to remind yourself of what you must do.
2. If options are presented, think about the choices of topics or approaches that will best enable you to display what you know. (Also, if you think you would *enjoy* writing one option more than another, choose it, because your writing will probably be more natural.)
3. Write down the audience for this paper. For whom are you writing? What are you trying to show that person? Try to visualize your audience in your mind.
4. Take time—maybe only five minutes—to jot down some notes and plans for yourself. Don't just start writing the first thing that comes into your head.
5. Look for an angle or plan of attack on your topic, some way to get into it that lets you write from your own perspective.
6. Let your knowledge of the topic structure your paper. You know the material. Think about what you know, how you want to write about it, and the audience for whom you are writing. In that way, you'll discover your angle or organization.

Writing

1. Take time, but not too much time. Write fairly rapidly, but don't let panic or nervousness make you write too quickly.

2. If you get stuck, keep on going. Don't waste time worrying about how to get around a writing block. Just move to the next item in your notes and come back to patch up the stuck place later.
3. Don't worry too much about "correctness," but be certain to leave yourself time to check your work later. If you get stuck trying to spell a word, choose another word with the same meaning that you *can* spell.
4. Once or twice as you write, look back at the examination question to make certain you are answering it and haven't drifted away from your purpose.
5. Once or twice as you write, look back at the audience you have chosen for the paper and visualize your reader(s) again.

Revision

1. At all costs, leave time for revision, even if it's only five minutes. People write strange things under the pressure of examinations, and they need to go back over their writing.
2. Ask yourself if you have answered the question. If not, look for places to insert a few lines to improve your answer.
3. Ask yourself whether any places sound awkward. (A good way to do this is to read the examination silently, mouthing the words.)
4. With two minutes or more to go, look over the paper with spelling, punctuation, and usage in mind. Correct anything obviously wrong or change it to something that seems right.

CONTENT WRITING
ACROSS THE CURRICULUM

There are, it seems to us, few limits to what can be accomplished by a single classroom teacher pursuing a content-area writing program for part or all of a school year. But it is self-evident that if students are to see writing as something valuable in all their schoolwork (and in later life), they must encounter interdisciplinary writing regularly, from kindergarten through twelfth grade. They must use writing as a tool for discovery and expression in all their subjects and come to understand or intuit its usefulness in any learning situation. With this in mind, a number of schools and districts in the United Kingdom, Canada, and the United States have begun developing something generally titled "A Policy of Writing Across the Curriculum." Evolved through faculty meetings and workshops as well as through in-service sessions, such policy statements outline each teacher's responsibility for developing writing skills. (Most statements are, in fact, broader than writing and include reading in the content areas as well. However, this discussion, will be limited to writing.)

We will not attempt to outline such a policy in this publication, because any statement must be hammered out and agreed upon by the people who will implement it. That task is not easy, for by no means do all teachers share the assumption that writing (and reading) must be a schoolwide concern. A statement, then, must take into consideration the concerns of teachers who feel they cannot teach writing successfully or who dismiss it as the responsibility of someone else—next year's or last year's teacher. Nor can the expectations in a policy statement be perceived as unreasonable by the cooperating teachers. Although it is quite practical for youngsters to do a bit of content writing in every class every day, to suggest it as a quota or even as a desirable goal may result in protests and the breakup of a writing-across-the-curriculum discussion.

Nevertheless, we do want to provide teachers with a model for a writing curriculum policy statement and then suggest how a school or district can go about implementing one.

Often at the secondary level the need for a writing across the curriculum policy will be identified by the English department (quite possibly with the support of the principal), and the first job becomes that of convincing teachers in other disciplines of the need for such a policy. At this point, the latter group needs to be reassured that English teachers are not simply passing the buck, shucking off their responsibility for teaching writing, and that the teaching of writing in the content areas need not be a horrendous additional burden. We suggest that the English department first make sure its own house is in order. (Is writing, in general, being taught well?) One way to start is to set an example by developing a policy for department members such as the following:

■ That English teachers broaden their scope to include at least one (two/three) content-area writing project(s) each semester, thus demonstrating that the English faculty cares about student writing in other subjects.

■ That English teachers see themselves as responsible for teaching the broad skills of written literacy—fluency, articulateness, a sense of purpose, a sense of audience—through frequent writing practice, both in the content areas and in connection with English/language arts subject matter. (Going a step further, the English department might set minimum levels of writing for its students—at a minimum, perhaps five or six carefully developed compositions each semester; ideally, something closer to the theme-a-week model proposed by Conant two decades ago.)

■ That English teachers use informal writing daily in their classes to reinforce and develop writing skills and to convey the idea that writing is an important tool for everyday use.

■ That English teachers continue to foster the idea, developed in the grades, that writing can and should be done in many diverse modes, imaginative as well as expository.

■ That English teachers learn about the content-area writing demands their students face in order to know accurately what their students are expected to do in other classes.

■ That English teachers teach students about the nature of the English language, especially dialects and usage, so that students are well informed about the facts of English usage and have a sense of how to take responsibility for the correctness of their own work.

■ That English teachers evaluate writing in terms of its content and substance, not just the quality of its language.

■ That the English department take responsibility for creating file folders of students' best writing as a way of promoting articulation among grade levels.

With such an English model before them, the subject teachers, in consultation with the English teachers, might develop some policy statements such as the following:

■ That subject teachers assign at least one (two/three/more) good, solid content-writing project(s) each semester.

■ That subject teachers cultivate the use of informal writing on a regular basis by having students keep journals, diaries, notebooks, logs, etc.

■ That subject teachers build writing excellence into criteria for evaluation in their courses.

■ That subject teachers take responsibility for clearly stating the specific conventions of writing in their disciplines so that students know exactly what they must do to write successfully for a specific teacher of a particular subject.

■ That subject teachers evaluate writing principally in terms of content but with genuine concern for quality as well.

■ That subject teachers teach "correctness" only as student errors genuinely interfere with communication and/or as they feel moved to take on this matter.

■ That subject teachers supply the English faculty with one piece of writing for each course indicative of the student's best writing.

In the end, no writing-across-the-curriculum policy statement will reflect a perfect or total consensus. Some teachers may regard the whole enterprise as a waste of time and refuse to participate; others may file away the policy statement and ignore it. But it has been our experience that schools willing to make the effort to develop the policy often find the writing program improved dramatically. Most faculty members will make an effort to adhere to the policy and to make it work. The amount of writing done in a school will quadruple, at least, and students in all classes will become more excited about and involved with their written work.

Some other suggestions for launching a writing-across-the-curriculum policy:

■ Include parents in the planning, letting them express their concerns about the quality of their children's writing. Also invite parents to participate in the literacy program, especially by serving as tutors or even as volunteer theme readers.

■ Start a pool of lesson plans and teaching ideas in the content areas as a catalyst for reluctant or cautious teachers.

■ Treat writing as a focus for in-service training for a year. Bring in writing consultants from a university or another school district and have them work on a long-range basis, helping develop the program, not simply making one-time presentations and departing.

■ Issue press releases on the concern for literacy to notify the community of the school's commitment.

■ Set up an annual school writing awards program.

■ Create a buddy system in which good writing teachers help subject teachers plan writing activities and consider ways and means of developing good lessons. (In exchange, subject teachers can help language arts teachers locate good subject matter materials for use in the English content-area writing program.)

■ Conduct an annual school- or systemwide writing week, in which students in all classes, elementary as well as secondary, focus on a common theme through writing. Present this writing and project work at a school- or districtwide writing fair. Invite parents and the media—they will love it.

PREPARING STUDENTS
FOR POSTSECONDARY EDUCATION

In simplest terms, we think that the kind of writing recommended in this publication, if done frequently by students under the sponsorship of at least some and preferably all of the teachers in a school, will go a long way toward successfully preparing students for postsecondary writing demands. The student who has experienced this kind of program will have written in many different discourse modes for a variety of audiences, and he or she will have seen how writing functions as a mode of discovery in many disciplines. Equally important, he or she should have a solid sense that writing is something one does regularly, that writing need not be an agonizing or painful task, that writing is a tool one can use constantly in academic studies.

Still, many responsible teachers want to do more. There are, after all, the constant complaints about students' writing skills. Can teachers prepare students specifically for postsecondary writing?

The answer, it seems to us, requires some doublethink: *yes* and *no.* *Yes*, one can do some specific training for postsecondary writing assignments. But, *no*, it is not possible to prepare students so completely for what they will face at a later time in their academic careers that it will come easily or smoothly for them. No matter how many content-area writing assignments teachers give, no matter how well they prepare their students, some of those students will come back after their first year in college saying, "You didn't get me ready for Professor Stamen's biology class."

We believe that a conscientious teacher should spend some time dealing directly with postsecondary preparation. Therefore we advocate a spring-of-the-senior-year program that would ideally take place in *each* class the student takes. Among the activities that we can recommend from our own experience:

■ Obtain samples of papers written in two- and four-year colleges and trade schools. (This is a useful project for last year's seniors who are away at school. Ask them to save their writing for a term.) Bring these papers into class and analyze them. What do postsecondary students write about? In what discourse forms? What kinds of comments do their instructors make on the papers? How would students in the class have handled the assignment? What other possibilities or approaches exist? This sort of "reality therapy" goes a long way toward preparing students by removing the mystery from future assignments. Further, it is often a highly motivating activity, for when students see how difficult some assignments and teachers can be, they are inclined to write with more fervor than ever before.

■ Invite college professors from various disciplines to meet with students and to describe their work. Although this project is not always possible in rural areas, most cities and towns are close enough to a four- or two-year college to make it feasible. Ask the professors to talk about their likes and dislikes in writing and, more important, to help students see how writing functions in a particular discipline as a way of exploring ideas and issues.

■ Bring back last year's seniors to hold a panel discussion on "survival in college." (Such a panel will invariably deal with such topics as dorm life, getting along with roommates, etc., but the teacher can bring it back to the focus on writing from time to time.)

■ Teach documentation and research procedures through several short papers rather than the conventional, massive research paper. As a matter of fact, surveys suggest that few postsecondary students write the traditional term paper—30 pages with 50 references and 42 footnotes. Although documentation and library skills are often required, most students are asked to write papers that express an idea or topic in just a few pages.

■ Finally, at the very end of the senior year, run a few simulated examination-writing sessions teaching or reinforcing the skills taught in the previous section. Choose topics that are college-like in nature and give them to students under blue-book conditions. One or two experiences of this sort will go a long way toward preparing students for the shock of their next year.

We want to close this section by reemphasizing our earlier assertion that postsecondary preparation should not dictate the secondary curriculum. The responsibility of the high school teacher is not, in our judgment, to prepare students for any eventuality they may face in their academic future. Rather, it is to prepare them as fully as possible in writing in the content areas, choosing subjects and audiences appropriate for the here and now, at the students' own level. If students write fluently and well, if they are comfortable with content-area writing, they will be highly adaptive to whatever set of expectations their next instructors may have for them.

PREPARING STUDENTS
FOR CAREER WRITING

College professors are not the only ones who complain about the inability of students to write: businesspeople frequently complain that the young people who come to them are not sufficiently literate. Too often the business view of literacy is limited to correct spelling;

nevertheless, such complaints have some validity. Because students do not write as much as they can and should in the schools, and because their writing is often limited to practice paragraphs in English class, they often flounder when given functional assignments by their bosses.

"Business English" and "Career Education" courses sometimes help supply the necessary literacy skills, but we think a good writing in the content area program can go further and provide all students—including those in college preparatory programs—an increased awareness of how writing functions outside the halls of academia. Our model for this approach is a very helpful book published by the National Association of Elementary School Principals entitled *The Yellow Pages of Learning Resources.* [16] The editor, Saul Wurman, observed that small towns and large cities are filled with learning resources seldom tapped by schools. Businesses and institutions can teach students all manner of practical skills, and so can the people who run them. Using Wurman's approach, students raise questions about what they would expect to learn at, say, an architect's studio, an airport, a hospital, a bakery. Then they visit these places and learn their lessons.

We adapt the model slightly by adding a *literacy component,* suggesting that students both study how writing is used in various businesses and occupations and put their findings in writing to share with their peers. In this way, students can practice writing the various forms required by the butcher, the baker, and the candlestick maker, thereby gaining a feel for real-world writing forms.

A community-based writing component can be built into almost any content-area writing project. Students studying entomology, for example, can talk to the insect control specialist at the county agent's office. If etymology is their concern, the local librarian or a college linguist can serve as a community resource. A class studying a historical era can discover a wide range of community members who share their interest and have memories or artifacts to share. Mathematics students can go into the field to study concepts in action in projects as diverse as bridge building or winterizing an automobile. Chemistry students can study as they watch doughnuts rise at the local bakery.

Community resources are available—it is simply a matter of recognizing how they can serve both the broad purposes of learning and the specialized purposes of teaching writing in the content areas.

SELECTED BIBLIOGRAPHY

1. Abruscato, Joe, and Hassard, Jack. *Loving and Beyond: Science Teaching for the Humanistic Classroom*. Pacific Palisades, Calif.: Goodyear Publishing Co., 1976.
2. Beck, James. "Theory and Practice of Interdisciplinary English." *English Journal* (February 1980): 28-32.
3. Bogojavlensky, Ann Rahnasto and others. *The Great Learning Book*. Menlo Park, Calif.: Addison-Wesley, 1977.
4. Delmar, P. Jay. "Composition and the High School: Steps toward Faculty-Wide Involvement." *English Journal* (November 1978): 36-38.
5. Edwards, Pat. "101 Ways to Publish Student Writing." In R.D. Walshe, ed., *Better Reading, Better Writing, Now*. Epping, New South Wales: Primary English Teaching Association, 1977.
6. Elbow, Peter. *Writing with Power*. New York: Galaxy, 1981.
7. Heck, Shirley. "Planning: The Key to Successful Interdisciplinary Teaching." *Kappa Delta Phi Record* (April 1979): 116-21.
8. Judy, Stephen. *The ABCs of Literacy*. New York: Oxford University Press, 1980.
9. Judy, Susan, and Judy, Stephen. *Gifts of Writing*. New York: Scribner's, 1980.
10. Lehr, Fran. "ERIC/RCS Report: Promoting Schoolwide Writing." *English Education* (Spring 1982): 47-51.
11. Maxwell, Rhoda, and Judy, Stephen. *Evaluating a Theme*. Rochester, Mich.: Michigan Council of Teachers of English, 1979. Also available from ERIC/RCS, 1111 Kenyon Rd., Urbana, IL 61801.
12. McLuhan, Marshall and others. *City as Classroom*. Agincourt, Ont.: Book Society of Canada, 1977.
13. Ruchlis, Hy, and Sharefkin, Belle. *Reality-Centered Learning*. New York: Citation Press, 1975.
14. Springer, Mark. "Science in the English Classroom." *English Journal* (October 1976): 35-36.
15. Summerfield, Geoffrey. *Topics in English*. London: Batsford, 1965.
16. Wurman, Saul, ed. *The Yellow Pages of Learning Resources*. Arlington, Va.: National Association of Elementary School Principals, 1972.